Information Literacy Landscapes

CHANDOS
INFORMATION PROFESSIONAL SERIES

Series Editor: Ruth Rikowski
(email: Rikowskigr@aol.com)

Chandos' new series of books are aimed at the busy information professional. They have been specially commissioned to provide the reader with an authoritative view of current thinking. They are designed to provide easy-to-read and (most importantly) practical coverage of topics that are of interest to librarians and other information professionals. If you would like a full listing of current and forthcoming titles, please visit our website www.chandospublishing.com or email info@chandospublishing.com or telephone +44 (0) 1223 891358.

New authors: we are always pleased to receive ideas for new titles; if you would like to write a book for Chandos, please contact Dr Glyn Jones on email gjones@chandospublishing.com or telephone number +44 (0) 1993 848726.

Bulk orders: some organisations buy a number of copies of our books. If you are interested in doing this, we would be pleased to discuss a discount. Please email info@chandospublishing.com or telephone +44(0) 1223 891358.

Information Literacy Landscapes

Information literacy in education, workplace and everyday contexts

ANNEMAREE LLOYD

Chandos Publishing
Oxford • Cambridge • New Delhi

Chandos Publishing
TBAC Business Centre
Avenue 4
Station Lane
Witney
Oxford OX28 4BN
UK
Tel: +44 (0) 1993 848726
Email: info@chandospublishing.com
www.chandospublishing.com

Chandos Publishing is an imprint of Woodhead Publishing Limited

Woodhead Publishing Limited
Abington Hall
Granta Park
Great Abington
Cambridge CB21 6AH
UK
www.woodheadpublishing.com

First published in 2010

ISBN:
978 1 84334 507 7

© A. Lloyd, 2010

British Library Cataloguing-in-Publication Data.
A catalogue record for this book is available from the British Library.

Typeset by Domex e-Data Pvt. Ltd.
Printed in the UK and USA.
Printed in the UK by 4edge Limited – www.4edge.co.uk

To see that all knowledge is a construction and that truth is a matter of context in which it is embedded is to greatly expand the possibilities of how to think about anything, even those we consider to be the most elementary and obvious.

Belenky, M., Clinchy, B., Goldberger, N., Tarule, J. (1986). *Women's ways of knowing: the development of self, voice and mind*, Basic Books, Harper & Collins, USA, p. 138.

Contents

About the author

Annemaree Lloyd is a senior lecturer at the School of Information Studies at Charles Sturt University where she teaches in the area of information literacy, information seeking and research methods. Her research interests focus on information literacy in theoretical and applied contexts, information literacy in the workplace, and digital contexts; information seeking and information behaviour; information skills; preservation practice, and lost and missing documentary heritage. Prior to joining the University Dr Lloyd worked as a Librarian and Library Manager in the vocational education and training sector. At University Dr Lloyd read sociology, political history and archaeology. Before retraining in librarianship, Dr Lloyd worked as an archaeologist.

Acknowledgements

No intellectual journey is taken alone and I have had the great good fortune to be have been accompanied by some wonderful people. These people have made the journey less lonely because of their willingness to engage in conversations that have challenged my views and who have provided me with a great deal of very good advice and much needed assistance. Marion Bannister and Sue Clancy travelled the road with me, not only giving me the courage to undertake this journey but also the benefit of their wisdom about the task of writing. Marion Bannister provided research and editorial assistance and I am forever grateful to her.

Various colleagues read chapters of the text as it was in preparation and I thank them from taking the time. Finally, my family is acknowledged with great love and thanks for giving me the time to undertake this work.

Foreword

For most people the term information literacy simply equates to the development of sound information skills, often in relation to the research process. Over the last three decades many volumes have been written on the subject as it has been operationalized. However, for me, information literacy means something different, and this is probably because I have not come to understand information literacy in the formal education context but through the study of workplace learning and of people as they engage with the multitude of practices and nuances that shape their workplace.

In my previous work as a vocational education librarian, I was concerned about why I could not get the apprentices in my own workplace to engage with good information literacy practices. I could not understand why they were not interested in learning the information literacy skills that I wanted to teach them. This situation puzzled me and eventually compelled me to undertake a doctoral study of information literacy in the workplace.

When I first began my study, I had every intention of studying the operationalized aspects of information literacy in the workplace (e.g. *defining*, *locating* and *accessing*), because this is what I had been taught that information literacy was. However, as my study progressed I began to understand that what we called information literacy in educational settings was different from what could be considered information literacy in the workplace—or in an everyday setting. It was only part of the information literacy equation. These differences fascinated me and led me to look for reasons why information literacy manifested in different ways. What I found in the workplace was a complexity that I had not anticipated. This complexity was underpinned by the different ways of learning that were available to workers, and more importantly, by the range of information sources and ways that information was used; sources that were not accounted for in the current conceptions of information literacy or in our practices as information literacy educators.

As my study progressed I also began to understand the critical role that other people play in the information literacy process. This led me to reassess information literacy not as the individual practice that librarians often think it is, but as a complex social practice: one that involves people co-participating in practices specific to their settings, and in the process, developing collective and common understandings, as they engage with knowledge that is heritaged through social, cultural, political and economic features that are laid down over time and through which practices are organized within a setting.

I also came to understand that becoming information literate was not only a textual practice, as we commonly conceive it to be in the library or educational setting. It was also linked to social information, which is tacit or nuanced in relation to workplace culture, or it may be derived from embodied sources that can never be articulated explicitly. This has led me to wonder, about the preparatory nature of educational institutions and to consider whether information literacy as it is currently conceived and taught in these institutions actually prepares people for life outside.

In writing this book, I hope to convey this complexity. At the very least, I hope that the message of this book is clear: information literacy is more complex than the sum of its skills. To understand this complexity we need to delve deeper into how information literacy practice is constructed through a range of landscapes and what social conditions influence that development.

Annemaree Lloyd

Introduction

Information literacy has been described as a core literacy and a prerequisite for lifelong learning in the twenty-first century (Garner, 2006). However, what is information literacy and how is it understood and played out in the multiple information settings that people are engaged in? Does being information literate in one context automatically mean being information literate in all? Can the complexity and richness of information literacy be described so that education, workplace and community sectors understand the processes that enable information literacy to occur?

Over the last 30 years our understanding of information literacy has developed generally within the context of formal learning. Here it is viewed as the users' relationship with text and technology (i.e. print and information and communication technologies literacy). However, as our research into information literacy proceeds and as we seek new landscapes to increase our knowledge of this phenomenon, we are increasingly beginning to understand that the practice of information literacy is not confined to formal learning information environments but is part of human activity in every landscape or context. Consequently, to understand information literacy requires more than an understanding of the student research process or the development and application of information skills, it requires a deep understanding of the complex social processes and arrangements that shape information and how it is used within any given context.

I believe that information literacy is a socio-cultural practice, one that is embedded and interwoven through the practices that constitute a social field (i.e. a context) and as such is subject to collaborative arrangements and activities. It is constituted by a set of interwoven understandings that guide interaction and is linked to the activities around information and knowledge sanctioned by any given setting. For example, the sayings and doings that order, enable and sometimes constrain activities will affect the way information is understood and shared in the construction of knowledge.

As a socio-cultural practice, information literacy is part of the ability of a fire fighter to 'speak a fire' or an Inuit to understand the complexity of the word 'snow'. It is also:

- the ability of an experienced artist to mix and remix colours to suit the palette of a masterpiece or of an ambulance officer to use his *gut* instincts built up over time to deal with a different or unexpected situation;

- understanding the technicalities of childbirth before it happens, but then really knowing it after;

- knowing the rules for soccer but not really knowing the game until you have played it.

- knowing what sources of information are relevant and necessary in developing the know-how or practical knowledge to perform a task and understanding the implications of this information experience after it occurs;

- knowing what co-participatory practices will inform your own performance in the workplace, and understanding what sources of information will shape your identity as a practitioner.

Information literacy acts as a catalyst to all types of learning, but the process of becoming information literate requires the whole person to be aware of themselves within the world (Csordas, 1994); to experience information through the opportunities that are furnished by the landscape or context; to recognize these experiences as contributing to learning; and, to take into account how the context and its sanctioned practices, sayings and doings enable and constrain information use. Information literacy gains its meaning not in the definition of its skills but through the way it manifests as a socio-cultural information practice in relation to the way people experience information and create meaning about this experience.

Becoming information literate requires a person to engage with information within a landscape and to understand the paths, nodes and edges that shape that landscape. Information landscapes are the communicative spaces that are created by people who co-participate in a field of practice. As people journey into and through these landscapes they engage with site-specific information. This engagement allows them to map the landscape, constructing an understanding of how it is shaped.

It is through this engagement that people, situate themselves within the landscape. In order to do so they develop information practices and undertake a range of activities that allows them to interrogate the sources of information within a setting. To undertake this journey into one's information landscape and to come to know it requires the act of becoming informed; i.e. to form an idea about the processes, practices and activities that are relevant to the learning that is required for that setting. Further, being informed allows members to understand and make judgements about these activities in the context of what is considered acceptable practice by others who share the same contextual space (e.g. a workplace or a classroom). All of these activities are significant for constructing knowledge.

Information can be explicit or it can be tacit. It can be accessed socially, corporeally (through the body) or through the written word, so that the person experiences, accesses and engages with different types of information in relation to the activities that are undertaken, e.g. reading, observing, talking, listening, reflecting, thinking or just doing. Over time, as these forms of information and ways of accessing information coalesce, this helps to fill in the framework for knowing about the nature of information within a particular setting. It helps explain how and why it is produced and reproduced, authorized, sanctioned, nuanced, applied and most importantly experienced.

The nature of this book

This book is for information literacy researchers, librarians and for educators who are interested in the ways people experience an information environment. It explores information literacy from a socio-cultural perspective as a situated 'informing' practice. In doing so, it draws from research in higher education, workplace and community settings for guidance about how information literacy occurs. It then uses this understanding to develop an architecture of information literacy practice that may be employed to inform research and pedagogy in educational, workplace and community training settings. This holistic approach allows us to conceptualize information literacy as it happens outside of preparatory settings rather than as often librarians and educators suppose it happens. It allows a rethinking of information literacy as a situated practice, one that treats not only the written word and codified knowledge as the legitimate sources, but also social and corporeal sources of information as central to becoming information literate. This approach conceptualizes the practice of information literacy as part of an integrated process that informs other practices, including learning the practice, and one that is in turn informed by it.

Therefore, information literacy can be considered as a meta-practice, one that occurs within social sites, which by its very nature is formed over time by collaboration with others. This produces shared practical understandings that are rich in historical, social, political and economic heritage. As a meta-practice information literacy needs to be analysed through the fields of practices that constitute a social site, suggesting that information literacy is context dependent. To understand this phenomenon, and to subsequently develop effective research architectures and pedagogy means that we need to identify the activities that constitute information practice. We need to understand how these activities are shaped and become integral to the setting through which they occur.

Aim of this book

The aim of this book is to encourage researchers and librarians to consider information literacy in broader terms, not only as a skill but in terms of how and why those skills manifest in specific ways as part of information practice. Information skills are not context-independent; they are established and sanctioned as part of the broader socio-cultural information practices of a community. Therefore, what this book attempts to do is to provide a framework for thinking about information literacy as a practice that enables people to engage with information in ways that will draw them into their communities.

Structure of this book

The idea that information literacy is a meta-practice is influenced by social and practice theory. In Chapter 2 these theories are briefly described and explored in order to orient the reader and to make the case for information literacy as a socio-cultural practice. The work of Theodore Schatzki (2001, 2002) provides the social ontology for this book, arguing that the social is 'a field of embodied, materially interwoven practice centrally organized around shared practical understandings' (2001, p. 3). This is an important underpinning for understanding information literacy as practice that is made visible according to the shared understandings of a community about what constitutes information and knowledge and which practices are considered legitimate. This section also introduces the work of Gregory Bateson (1972) who has argued that information, in order to be understood as information, has to be perceived by the user as making a difference. This understanding of information fits well with a socio-cultural perspective that focuses attention towards the way people make meaning through their interactions with others and in the context of their settings.

The scope of research that has been conducted in the higher education, workplace and community landscapes will be discussed in Chapters 3 (higher education), 4 (workplace) and 5 (community). It will be evident from each of these chapters that there are different ways of thinking about information literacy. This serves to illustrate that the practice has a deep and rich level of complexity driven by complex social factors that give the settings their shape and character. These factors need to be removed in layers so that we can understand why the practice manifests itself in different ways in different contexts.

Chapter 6 will continue to explore the concept of an information landscape in relation to the three landscapes that have been discussed.

An architecture for information literacy practice presented in Chapter 7 is the first step towards this understanding. This chapter will also present a number of sensitizing concepts that encourage researchers and practitioners to think about information literacy holistically in each of the settings, rather than as a skills-based literacy. Thereby an understanding will be achieved of what drives information literacy practice in each of them. The idea that information skills are generic and transferable is debatable. Studies in the workplace (Lloyd, 2005, 2007; Hepworth and Smith, 2008) have begun to demonstrate that they have different requirements to higher education where information literacy is generally taught as part of the student assignment and/or research process. By understanding what drives a setting, we are in turn in a position to understand what skills are common and what skills are specific to each sector. A recent skills survey for Microsoft (Swabey, 2007) reported in *Information Age* indicates information literacy and information and communication technology skills are currently ranked seventh of 12 in those skills required by business. This will rise to second place by the year 2017. This is a sobering figure, one that we need to pay full attention to if we are going to prepare people to be effective workplace practitioners and full participants in civil society. However, while we continue to impose a library-centric view on the information literacy skills debate, we will find that we continue to lack relevance to the world outside of librarianship.

If we as librarians and information literacy educators are really serious about information literacy and about increasing our influence both inside and outside the education sector then it is time for us to understand the nature of information literacy and how information literacy is conceived in other settings. It will be vital for us to know which information skills are valued and use this knowledge to develop information literacy programmes that have relevance to employees and employers alike.

References

Bateson, G. (1972). *Steps to an ecology of the mind.* San Francisco, CA: Jason Aronson Inc.

Csordas, T. (1994). *Embodiment and experience: the existential ground of culture and self.* Cambridge: Cambridge University Press.

Garner, S. D. (2006). *High-level colloquium in information literacy and lifelong.* Report of a meeting sponsored by the United Nations Educational, Scientific and Cultural Organisation (UNESCO), National Forum on Information Literacy (NFIL) and the International Federation of Library Associations and Institutions (IFLA). Bibliotheca Alexandrina. Alexandria, Egypt, November 6–9, 2005. Retrieved August 2008, from http://archive.ifla.org/III/wsis/High-Level-Colloquium.pdf/.

Hepworth, M. and Smith, M. (2008). Workplace information literacy for administrative staff in higher education. *Australian Library Journal,* 57(3), 212–236.

Lloyd, A. (2005). Information literacy; different contexts, different concepts, different truths? *Journal of Librarianship and Information Science,* 37(2), 82–88.

Lloyd, A. (2007). Recasting information literacy as sociocultural practice: implications for library and information science researchers. Paper presented at the Sixth International Conference on Conceptions of Library and Information Science: Featuring the Future, Boras, Sweden. Retrieved 12 December, from http://InformationR.net/ir/12-4/colis/colis34.html/.

Schatzki, T. (2001). The practice turn. In *The practice turn in contemporary theory* (pp. 1–14). London: Routledge.

Schatzki, T. (2002). *The site of the social: a philosophical account of the constitution of social life and change.* Pennsylvania, PA: Pennsylvania University Press.

Swabey, P. (2007). IT skills failing to ignite business success [Electronic Version]. *Information Age.* Accessed 12 December 2008 from http://license.icopyright.net/user/viewFreeUseact?fuid=NzU3Odly/.

2

Conceptual orientation

Introduction

The purpose of this chapter is to orientate the reader to the concept of information literacy as a socio-cultural practice. It introduces a number of ideas and theories that influence my understanding of information literacy, which can be considered here as constructionist. Constructionism focuses on collective reality whereby meaning is produced and organized through 'shared understandings, practices and language' (Schwandt, 2003, p. 305).

This chapter is divided into a number of sections; the first section will briefly introduce the concepts of landscapes, information and literacy; concepts that may already be familiar to many readers. This orientation will also serve to introduce the central concepts that inform a constructionist understanding (i.e. situated practice) communities of practice and practice theories. The chapter will conclude with a synthesis of these ideas.

What is an information landscape?

Throughout this book I will use the term 'information landscape' to describe the broad contexts or settings through which information literacy has been researched. In Chapter 6, I will explore the concept of the information landscape in more detail. For the moment I will use this term to describe the communicative space through which people develop identities and form relationships based on shared practices and ways of doing and saying things. Information landscapes are intersubjectively created spaces that have resulted from human interaction, in which information is created and shared and eventually sediments as knowledge. Consequently as an information landscape (just like a physical landscape) evolves, its social, historical, political and economic *layers* are deposited to form the foundations of the intersubjective space. Information landscapes are colonized by the particular values, beliefs, understandings and ways of doing things that represent the interaction between people as they co-participate. Therefore these spaces are 'imbued with symbolic value which, in turn, can generate strong attachments' (Warmsley and Lewis, 1984, p. 159), which work to enact and constrain participation within a community of practice. Explicitly, these spaces are characterized by the signs, symbols, artefacts, sayings and doings that define these spaces to its members and identify the boundaries of the environment to outsiders. To become an insider requires access to information that is valued and sanctioned within that space, allowing interrogation, interpretation and mapping of information. This requires knowing about the sources of information that will inform practice, why they are valued and sanctioned by the community, how they are nuanced and the ways in which they can be accessed.

Information and literacy

The lack of a single definition of *information* reveals the broad and complex nature of the term. Buckland's (1991, p. 351) statement that definitions of information may 'not be fully satisfactory' underlies the multiple realities of the term and suggests that how information is understood will be a reflection of the context in which the phenomenon is being explored and defined.

Similar problems plague the definition of *information literacy*. Cheuk (2002) has argued that information literacy suffers from the combining of two problematic terms, information and literacy. It therefore seems prudent in a book about information literacy to very briefly discuss what I understand as the meaning of these two terms before moving to current definitions of information literacy in Chapter 3.

What is information?

There are many definitions and typologies (Dervin, 1976; Buckland, 1991) of information and I do not intend to spend a great deal of time exploring these. To do so could take an entire book (and has); however, for those interested in this area, Case (2007) is a good starting point. Definitions of information tend to fall into two major categories that are influenced by the major paradigms in research: positivism (or scientific method) and interpretivism. About the first, positivism, it is enough to say that information is conceptualized as a tangible objective entity. From this rationalist perspective, information is 'out there' and is something to be discovered and understood in similar ways by any number of people.

This book takes a socio-cultural approach, which from a library and information science perspective emphasizes the relationship between people, focusing on their experiences with information and the subjective and intersubjective meaning that is constructed from this experience. Drawing from ecological theory, Bateson (1972, p. 453) suggests 'information is any difference which makes a difference'. The difference that Bateson refers to is an 'abstract matter' (Bateson, 1972, p. 458) that changes once it is perceived by an individual as being useful or even unhelpful. From this ecological perspective information is transformative, because to receive or interact with information is to transform (even in the smallest sense) to become different. Davenport and Prusak (2000, p. 3) echo the perspective of Bateson when they suggest that 'information is meant to change the way the receiver perceives something, to have an impact on his judgement and behaviour. It must inform; it's data that makes a difference'. To understand how knowledge is constructed it is important to understand how an individual interacts with one of the basic building blocks—information and the process of gathering information. Interacting with and experiencing information produces a change in the individual (for better or worse) and this change contributes to a person's ability to construct knowledge. Therefore, people determine what information is and decide on its relevance in relation to what they can action by drawing upon, contesting or ignoring. When a person recognizes data as useful it becomes information, and in the process of this selection a *difference* is made. Bateson's definition of information is also employed by Case (2007) who suggests information has both external and internal influences that must be perceived. According to Case (2007) information 'can be any difference you perceive, in your environment or within yourself. It is any aspect that you notice in the pattern of reality' (p. 5).

Ruben (1992) characterizes information as a process that is 'transformed and configured for use by a living system' (p. 22). He attempts to capture the idea of information in three 'orders'. The environmental order is characterized by external stimuli (such as messages) that require our attention. The second 'order' is information that has a subjective quality in that it is our internalized representation of the world. The third order is derived from information that is 'socially constructed, negotiated, validated, sanctioned and/or privileged appropriations, representations and artefacts' (Ruben, 1992, p. 23).

Cornelius (2004) suggests that information is a *social product* affected within a social context and is constituted through symbols, action and language as a social construction of the context. Information contributes to this construction by enabling a person to become informed about content, about practice, about social values, about the socially produced structures and the organizations of a setting, about what is morally and ethically right, and about what is wrong.

Information can be understood as the basis for human interaction—for everyday existence, for learning, working and playing. However, it is not meaningful to us in its abstract form (as data). Information needs to be situated within a context in order for it to have meaning and to be used in meaningful ways by people. In this respect, information is not static or objectively available; it is the product of a negotiated construction between individuals interacting with the artefacts, texts, symbols, actions and in consort with other people in context.

The transformation of data into information is an active process that is influenced by our situated experiences. This in turn produces knowing, which according to Wenger (1998), is 'defined only in the context of specific practices, where it arises out of the combination of a regime of competence and an experience of meaning' (p. 141). It is through the situated dialogic relationship that information is transformed into knowledge. Talja (1997) highlights an important point when she suggests that knowledge (the stuff that is produced when information is contextualized) can only be legitimized according to discourses of practice. She states: 'knowledge consists of a mix of scientific or expert knowledge, and unconscious, selective or culture-specific background assumptions. In certain social contexts and within certain social interests these assumptions appear factual or valid, where in other social contexts they are seen as questionable.' (p. 73).

To summarize, how we view information will depend on our epistemological influence (e.g. whether we see information as objective and discoverable or whether we see it as situated and dialogic, and constituted through experience). From my own perspective it is the second conceptualization that provides the description of 'information' in the term information literacy.

What is literacy?

Like information, there are many definitions and discourses that surround the concept of *literacy*, each drawing from different theoretical perspectives and understandings and again it is beyond the scope of this book to explore or problematize these in depth. Searle (2003) argues that there is 'no universally accepted definition of literacy' (p. 52) and suggests that the reason for this lies in the way the relationship between literacy and learning is viewed (p. 52). These perspectives are briefly discussed in this section.

When a *cognitive* perspective is adopted, literacy will be seen in relation to *functional* literacy, as a capability that enables an individual to acquire knowledge and skills in reading and writing. Often referred to as the autonomous view of literacy, this approach focuses on the individual and suggests that literacy has no spatial or temporal boundaries, and is context free. Reading and writing are understood in this model to be generic basic skills that can be benchmarked and measured.

From a *technicist* perspective, literacy is understood to be a 'tool or conduit for performance, a means of encoding and decoding information, a generic skill or key competency' (Searle, 2003, p. 61). Critics of this approach often argue that this perspective results in a 'bolted on' approach to literacy whereby literacy is viewed as a *competency* that is transferable across different contexts.

The view of literacy as a *social practice* that is espoused by Searle (2003) emphasizes that: 'reading, writing and enunciating are cultural practices that are learnt in specific cultural contexts which have epistemological significance' (Searle, 2003, p. 61). This means context and relationships will influence how literacy is used and how people are socialized into the context. Literacy is viewed as a socially and historically construed practice that cannot be generalized across cultures, or treated as neutral or as technical, because it is subject to power relationships within a culture. In the same vein Tuominen *et al.* (2005) suggest that literacies are connected 'to historically and contextually defined social values and technologies' (p. 337). Consequently, within any setting or context, there will be literacies that are authorized and some that are not. For Tuominen *et al.* (2005, p. 337), literacy essentially means 'being able to enact in practice the rules of argumentation and reasoning that an affinity group in a specific knowledge domain considers good or eloquent'.

The emergence of the concept of *multiliteracies*, which focus not only on text, but also on visual, audio, spatial and electronic mediums, has recently begun to challenge the autonomous and technical views of literacy. With a focus on 'designs of meaning', multiliteracies move beyond textual domains to recognize the multiple domains in which an individual operates and through which a person engages with meaning making. This approach recognizes the need to explore beyond the economic imperative and the production of knowledge workers—to move towards understanding how multiple ways of knowing are produced through the different domains in which an individual is situated. The emphasis within this perspective is on situatedness and plurality and the influence of power on developing literacy (Searle, 2003).

Adopting a *critical literacy* approach to literacy and to information literacy, Elmborg (2006) recognizes that literacy is a socio-cultural practice that reflects the ideological positions of a community and is, therefore, influenced by the power and control that certain groups have over the production, reproduction and distribution of information. He contends that: 'people produce, read, and interpret texts in communities, not in isolation. Communities reach consensus about interpretation, sometimes easily and sometimes contentiously. Literacy cannot be described, therefore, in broad terms as a set of universal skills and abstract processes. Rather, literacy is in constant flux and embedded in cultural situations, each situation nuanced and different from others' (p. 193).

The variations in conceptions of literacy suggest that, like the concept of information, literacy is not simply a set of decontextualized skills that can be codified, measured and audited. Rather, literacy refers to a range of highly contextual social practices in which people engage. Literacy, just like the concept of information, is influenced by the ideology of the community through which the practice is interpreted.

Practice theory, situated learning and communities of practice

It is impossible to talk about information literacy without talking about learning as the two are inextricably entwined. Therefore, this book also draws on theories of *practice* and *learning* in order to situate information literacy as a socio-cultural practice, as it is constituted through participation in education, working and everyday life. Consequently, the concept of situated learning and communities of practice are also important, as is the theory development of practice theorists.

Practice theory

Practice theories emphasize ways of engaging with the world and are concerned with exploring human activity, subjectivity, intersubjectivity, embodiment, language and power in relation to the 'organization, reproduction and transformation of social life' (Schatzki, 2001, p. 1). Inherent in this focus is a concern about information (as a socially constructed phenomenon) and how an experience with information produces and reproduces outcomes that are specific and sanctioned by the social settings in which a person lives, works or plays.

Developing an understanding of practice and practice theory is an important step in conceptualizing how information literacy functions as a socio-cultural practice. Because information literacy is a meta-practice embedded within all other practices, it therefore manifests as a socially discursive practice in ways that are ascribed by the setting. As a practice, information literacy makes learning possible by connecting users to various modalities of information that are situated within a social site. This allows people to access, interrogate, interpret and reflect on information in a process of meaning making that will eventually connect them to the shared knowledge of the field in which they participate. As a practice that is socially and culturally influenced, information literacy needs to be understood in the context of the information landscape that is shaped by its discourses, and practices that enable some forms of information, while constraining other forms.

By producing an account of how different types of information and subsequently knowledge is produced and reproduced, practice theory can offer a more holistic approach to understanding information literacy as a practice that acts as a catalyst for learning.

What is a practice?

While practice theory might be unfamiliar to the library and information science sector it has influenced the writing of many influential theorists whose work reflects on human activity, subjectivity, intersubjectivity, meaning making, rationality, embodiment, production and reproduction, power and the transformation of social life (Schatzki, 2001, p. 1). There is no unified approach or definition of practice and, in general, most practice theorists are sceptical about theories that claim to deliver explanations about social life (Schatzki, 2001, p. 4). Consequently, explications of practice differ depending on the epistemological orientation and interest of the enquirer. The origins of practice theory can be traced back to philosophers, such as Aristotle, and to more recent work by Wittgenstein (1958) and Dreyfus (1991). In the field of social theory, the work of theorists such as Bourdieu (1984), Giddens (1984) and Schatzki (2001) has been prominent. Bourdieu theorized practice as interwoven activities that were integrated into a field of practice and attempted to clarify the idea through the central principle of habitus, i.e. 'a stable system of dispositions and structures which generate and organize practices' (Bourdieu, 1984, p. 54). Giddens (1984) provides an account of practice whereby practice is rendered visible by a group of actions governed by rules and constituted through situated activities and interactions, which are influenced by the agency of other actors.

While each approach to practice theory produces different accounts of what constitutes practice, Schatzki (2001, pp. 2–3) reports that most practice theorists agree that practices are constituted through arrays of human activity that produce, among members engaged in the practice, a shared account of embodied know-how or practical understanding. For Schatzki (2002), whose interests lie in understanding how social life is constituted and transformed, a practice is a meaningful bundle of activities and constellation of actions (p. 71), which are interwoven to form the practice. According to this author, practice embraces 'sayings, doings and tasks' (p. 73). By this, he means what is spoken or gestured of and about (sayings), what is performed and enacted (doings) and how these enactments and performance are legitimized and the outcomes they produce. He suggests that 'a practice always exhibits a set of ends that participants should or may pursue, ... and a selection of tasks that they should or may perform ... (p. 80)'. However, he also suggests that these may not always be regular or routine because they are situated within contexts and therefore need to accommodate the unique or unexpected events that can occur, even within the context of everyday practice.

Any account of practice must not only recognize the cognitive, but the teleoaffective (how things are done and why), as this dimension also influences the way practice will proceed in a given setting (Schatzki, 2002). Therefore, accounts of practice must also acknowledge the affective and embodied elements that are constituted by the whole person experiencing the rules (formal and informal) and the shared practical understandings that are intersubjectively constituted within a setting.

Practices are relational and therefore social in nature and are formed, over time, through an intra-group dialogic process. They are not constituted as an individual activity, but rather, are located within and through group activities allowing the individual to become enacted into the group and the profession. This suggests that there is an intersubjective aspect to the concept, its dimensions and arrangements, which facilitate the development of shared understanding and shared skills (Schatzki, 2001). In writing about practice as the property of groups, Kemmis (2006, p. 2) suggests that they are 'shaped through histories and traditions that locate practices in such a way that they are "inherited" already formed, by contemporary practitioners, who in their turn, become the custodians and developers of practices'. Therefore, practices are organized and conducted according to the discourses that characterize and shape a setting. These might include educational discourse, the discourse of specific workplaces, religious discourse, or even informing discourse, which would direct what information is considered valid. Kemmis' argument supports the work of Schatzki (2002) who suggests that practices are prefigured (enabled or constrained by the context) and this prefiguration is the product of social interaction that over time creates layers of meanings in relation to practices and activities.

The concept of practice as a social activity is also central to practice theorists who acknowledge that skill development underpins the maintenance of practice, and requires a shared understanding of embodied knowledge or know-how (Schatzki, 2002). For Wenger (1998), practice is an activity that is driven by a constellation of influences that have developed over time, shaping the community and its character. According to Wenger (1998, p. 47) 'practice connotes doing, but not just doing in itself. It is doing in a historical and social context that gives structure and meaning to what we do. In the sense, practice is always social'. Practice is represented (1) explicitly through language, tools, documents, images, roles, etc., and (2) tacitly through activities that cannot be articulated (e.g. cues, embodied understandings, sensitivities, perceptions, tricks of the trade).

Bodies in practice

Acknowledging the whole person in information literacy practice, suggests that we not only understand practices related to text or social access and dissemination of information, we also need to understand the role of the body in practice and constituted through practice. As Wenger (1998, p. 49) suggests, '... practice is practice. Things have to be done, relationships worked out, processes invented, situations interpreted, artefacts produced, conflicts resolved. We may have different enterprises, which give our practices different characters. Nevertheless, pursuing them always involves the same kind of embodied, delicate, active, social, negotiated, complex process of participation.'

Practice can therefore be characterized as consisting of a number of elements that are entwined. Reckwitz (2002, p. 243) lists these as 'forms of bodily activities, forms of mental activities, "things" and their use, a background knowledge in the form of understanding, know-how, states of emotion and motivational knowledge'. Schatzki (2002, p. 3) suggests that the body is the 'common meeting point of mind and activity'. This understanding writes the body into understanding practice and as we shall see later on in this book, corporeal information (i.e. of the body) is integral for understanding information literacy.

Therefore, accounting for the body in practice is central to practice theory. Reckwitz (2002, p. 250) suggests that a practice is a 'routinized way in which bodies are moved, objects are handled, subjects are treated, things described and the world is understood'. Central to his understanding of practice is the role of the body in practice, which gives the 'world of humans its visible orderliness' (p. 251).

Consequently, themes of the body as an agent of practice are also introduced as part of an account of information literacy and underpin the notion of the *whole body* acting in the wider world (Csordas, 1994). Bodies play a central role in this construction; as a source of sensory and sentient information, as an instrument of non-verbal communication and a symbol of community and professionals, bodies reflect the discourse in which the person is situated socially, politically and historically.

Corporeal information is critical for the construction of meaningful practice. Merleau-Ponty (1962) suggests that bodies become storehouses of information and understandings that find a commonality of shared meaning within a specific community or culture. Accounting for the body in the construction of knowledge, Dewey (1938) emphasized that the *social body* and the sociality of experience through bodily interaction, leads to shared conceptions between people. The role of the body as critical in the generation of information was also recognized by Goffman (1983) who saw that as an information source, the body provided visual clues about roles and practices. The importance of the body in, and as part of, learning is echoed by McClelland *et al.* (2002, p. 4) who suggest that: 'We are to the world as body. The lived body is more than the body alone; it connotes the integration of the physical body, mind consciousness, and how we are in the world. We have no consciousness and no learning without bodies. Understood this way, learning is a bodily affair …'.

Common threads in practice theory

Theories of practice emphasize a number of things. First, that knowledge is relational, that is, knowledge (or as I prefer knowing) is a phenomenon that is brought about by engaging with the discourses, practices, and tools of a setting. Central to this engagement is interaction with others who are participating in practice within a particular setting. These settings are shaped and influenced by 'practices built up over time', which means that they have a trajectory of social, historical and political influences that drive practice within the setting (Wenger, 1998; Schatzki, 2002).

These theories also emphasize the process of making meaning as a negotiation between people who are situated and participating in a particular setting. This leads to the production and reproduction of identity and ways of interacting and engaging with the world (Wenger, 1998). Meaning comes from the process of negotiation, and at the core of this process is information (the phenomenon being negotiated) that is drawn from sites of knowledge that are valued by the particular group. These sites of knowledge shape and characterize specific communities (e.g. workplace, scholarly or sporting communities) and the people who practice within it; therefore, they are transformative, producing and reproducing specific identities (e.g. fire fighters, teachers, musicians, students and sports people).

Even though there is no unified theory of practice, Schatzki (2002) notes there are a number of common points of agreement among theorists. These are:

- that, at minimum, all practice approaches are understood as suites of activity;
- knowledge is relational and, therefore, constructed and is brought about by engaging with discourses, other practices, and tools of a particular setting;
- practices have a social, historical and political trajectory (i.e. they are built up over time);
- meaning making is a negotiation between people in a particular setting, leading to the production and reproduction of identity and

ways of interacting. An important aspect of the meaning making is the ability to contest information about practice; and

- understanding practice requires us to focus on more than just the internalized processes, it also requires us to understand embodied performance.

Communities of practice

Much has been written about communities of practice (e.g. Brown *et al.*, 1989; Lave and Wenger, 1991; Wenger, 1998; Brown and Duguid, 2001). This construct is useful in accounts of how information literacy manifests itself and is constituted as a socio-cultural practice. People learn as they participate in situ. They learn not only about the actual performance of practice (e.g. the doing of practice), but also they also engage with nuanced and tacit information (e.g. the saying of practice). This latter form of information is coded and specific to the community who determine what practices and knowledge are legitimate. This type of information reflects the history, assumptions, beliefs, values and rules that allow new members to learn about and eventually become members of a community. In the process of learning, people interact with the tools of practice (objects, signs, technologies and language) and the activities that define group practices and signify membership. Through these interactions they engage and are introduced to the information modalities and information activities that are sanctioned and legitimized by the community. This experience of information is managed and directed by experienced members of the group and has a twofold purpose. First, it enables new members to engage with the coded information that will enable the formation of a recognizable and acceptable identity that reflects knowledge about practice as it is understood by the community. Secondly, by introducing new members to sanctioned ways of knowing, the community ensures the maintenance of group culture and tradition, enabling new members to develop a sense of place.

A community of practice is often cited (e.g. Lave and Wenger, 1991; Wenger, 1998) as the exemplar for understanding the tacit, implicit and coded processes that underpin becoming informed about practice. These processes include the sanctioning of legitimate information, the creation of knowledge and mutual understanding, and the shaping and enacting of identity. Newcomers are furnished with opportunities to connect with nuanced understandings or coded information. As they continue developing and negotiating their relationships with other members, they learn how to decode this information and are thus drawn into full membership as they become old hands or experts. Lave and Wenger (1991, p. 98) define communities of practice in the following way:

> A community of practice is a set of relations among persons, activity and the world, over time and in relations with other tangential and overlapping communities of practice. A community of practice is an intrinsic condition for the existence of knowledge, not least because it provides the interpretive support necessary for making a sense of its heritage. This, participation in the cultural practice in which any knowledge exists is an epistemological principle of learning. The social structure of this practice, its power relations, and conditions for legitimacy define possibilities for learning (i.e. legitimate peripheral participation).

Communities of practice are constituted by a 'rapid flow of information' between members about the meaning of practice, enterprise, identity, mutual engagement and the sharing of artefacts (Wenger, 1998, p. 125). The sharing of this bond and narrative is brought about by common endeavour and collaborative socio-technical practices that are shared across distributed sites within a field of practice (Gee, 2000), and understood as the 'total nexus of interconnected human practices' (Schatzki, 2001, p. 2).

While communities of practice are often described in romantic and unproblematic terms, they can also be viewed as sites that constrain the sharing of information. The contestability of practice has been recognized by Brown and Duguid (2001, p. 198), who employ communities of practice as their unit of analysis for examining the flow of knowledge in an organization. These authors suggest that communities of practice can create *epistemic differences* that effectively create barriers between different groups within complex organizations and thus affect the flow of information.

The construct of communities of practice is central for understanding information literacy as a socio-cultural practice and provides yet another layer of complexity. Communities of practice facilitate access to tacit information that cannot be articulated through text. As such they create powerful information landscapes that 'enhance or constrain participation by opening or closing opportunities for observation, mentoring, guidance and collaborative work' (Tennant, 1999, p. 173).

In a community of practice, developing a shared understanding about what constitutes information is as important as the information itself. As a social site, a community of practice plays a critical role in the meaning making process that occurs when people engage with information that informs their practical understanding (embodied knowledge), along with information that allows them to decode the cultural constitution of a group (socially nuanced information). This engagement is a two-way flow; newcomers are drawn into practice, by the sharing of information that will facilitate the development of intersubjectivity (shared understanding). This connects newcomers with key concepts, ideas and procedures that have relevance and are valued by the community as its collective practice facilitates the shaping and reshaping of identity. It also allows old timers (or experts) to draw from newcomers, salient information about new practices that may in turn inform or enhance current practice. This sharing of information occurs through the affordances of situated learning, which will be discussed in the next section.

Situated learning

The concept of situated learning is also an important feature of practice theory and for information literacy, emphasizing learning, not as an internalized and individualistic practice but as a socially situated practice where 'agent, activity and the world mutually constitute each other' (Lave and Wenger, 1991, p. 33). In situated learning the cerebral is not privileged, rather emphasis is focused towards social interaction through participation, as an essential but often invisible part of information sharing within a social setting. The concept of situated learning accounts for the dynamic and changing nature of knowledge as a product of ongoing systems of activity that are socially, historically and culturally constituted. That is, it is anchored within context. It promotes a view of knowing that is localized and specific to context and 'where activities, tasks and functions, and understandings do not exist in isolation; they are part of broader systems of relations in which they have meaning' (Lave and Wenger, 1991, p. 53).

Learning from a social practice perspective is dynamic and involves interaction and participation, a situation whereby a person is defined through their relations to community systems of meaning. In learning about a new setting, newcomers engage with information sources and practices that are sanctioned and legitimized by more experienced old timers in the setting. Through this engagement learning occurs and along with it a transition as they begin the process of shaping and reshaping their identities. Lave and Wenger (1991) suggest that 'learning thus implies becoming a different person with respect to the possibilities enabled by these systems of relations' (p. 53).

Lave and Wenger (1991) argue this best when they suggest that learning is a situated activity and a generative social practice whereby the person participates in practice and in that the process produces and reproduces them as part of a community of practice. They suggest that 'a person's intentions to learn are engaged and the meaning of learning is configured through the process of becoming a full participant in a socio-cultural practice. This social process includes, indeed subsumes, the learning of knowledgeable skills' (Lave and Wenger, 1991, p. 29).

Learning is, therefore, characterized by practice theory as social, occurring through participation and the continually evolving and renewing of relations between people, actions and the world.

Information practice research in library and information science

Although the concept of information practice, is still emerging in the library and information science field, it has gradually been made visible in information research by those who are interested finding an 'alternative to the dominant concept of information behaviour' (Savolainen, 2007, p. 119). While information behaviour research tends to focus on the *individual*, information practice research is more focused towards the *domain or community* as the unit of analysis. According to Talja (2006, p. 123) studies on information practice represent 'a more sociologically and contextually oriented line of research' with most researchers drawing from a constructionist perspective. This perspective emphasizes the collective, discursive and intersubjective nature of interaction and knowledge production, rather than the subjective and motive-based focus often favoured by information behaviour researchers. Consequently, the term information practice is preferred over 'information behaviour' because it acknowledges the social and cultural dimensions that influence all practices, including information practice.

Where a constructionist perspective is adopted (McKenzie, 2003; Talja and Hansen, 2005; Talja, 2006; Johannisson and Sundin, 2007) emphasis is placed on 'social practices, the concrete and situated activities of interacting people, reproduced in routine social contexts across time and space' (Savolainen, 2007, p. 122). This approach is particularly relevant for understanding information literacy as a practice that is constituted through a constellation of information activities. However, a particular issue for this field relates to the definition of information practice with few researchers attempting deeper reflection on the meaning of the term. This often leads to terms such as information behaviour, information seeking and information practice being used interchangeably to denote the same operationalized activity (Savolainen, 2007). Choo (2007) who has examined information seeking in organizations clearly defines information practice as 'repeated patterns of behavior that affirm organizational roles, structures, and forms of interaction. Information practices are revealed in the activities by which people find, use and share information to do their work and sustain their identities.' However, Johannisson and Sundin (2007) advocate the term social practice to define an institutionalized activity that encompasses formal rules, including rules about information seeking.

Connecting practice and information literacy

As a practice, information literacy can be characterized as a constellation of activities (e.g. information seeking, sharing of information) and skills (e.g. information searching, evaluating and organizing). These activities and skills are sanctioned within a particular environment and will legitimize some forms of information and ways of knowing, while at the same time contesting others.

To participate in practice requires us, at the very foundation of practice, to: (1) access and use information; (2) experience it through negotiation with others; (3) produce and reproduce it through activity; (4) be influenced by it; or (5) make decisions about how to act on it (i.e. to construct knowledge), to accept or contest it. To do this we need to situate our minds and bodies within context, we need to actively engage and act on the types of information that are available and relevant to us and are recognized as valuable to others who are engaged in similar practices.

As a socio-cultural practice, information literacy is more than just the ability to acquire a set of skills or an understanding of their application or execution. To become information literate requires an increasingly complex rich and nuanced understanding of the social, textual and corporeal modalities of information—how these modalities are constituted, and how they are nuanced, contested and afforded. Understanding information literacy as a situated, socially constituted information practice also allows us to account for the relationships between identity formation and information, because it is through access to appropriate information sources that our intersubjective 'selves' are formed. This arises from the reflective experience of information that occurs when people come together in practice and over time come to see themselves as practitioners.

Experiencing information is not merely a matter of acquiring or transmitting information nor is it a matter of simply reproducing or repackaging it in a way that is measurable. Understanding the nature of information literacy, as a catalyst for learning, requires us to account for the experience of information inside and outside of the body. It also requires us to recognize that this experience is not just a cerebral activity, but an activity that requires the whole body to participate in practices that are situated. A consistent theme that will run through this book is that current conceptions of information literacy do not account for the power of the phenomenon as a catalyst for learning. If information literacy is to be viewed as the core literacy that underpins other literacies, then we need to be able to understand how the phenomenon reveals itself across a range of contexts, and the outcomes that are produced as people experience information.

Therefore, this book is unashamedly contextualist, and I will argue information literacy should be viewed as practice that is subject to social processes, which in turn are influenced by the concerns and interests of people and communities as they practise within any given context. As a socio-cultural practice that is constituted through a web of interconnected activities, information literacy needs to be understood in relation to the experiences with information that occur when people connect with the signs, symbols and others in consort. It also needs to be understood in the context of the transition this experience produces.

Conceptualizing information literacy

Brown *et al.* (1989, p. 247) make an important point about concepts, when they argue that concepts should not be viewed as self-contained entities, but rather as tools that can only be understood through use.

As you read the various chapters of this book, I hope you will come to understand that my conceptualization of information literacy is much broader and may seem at odds with our current library-based conceptions of the phenomenon. The reason for this is that my research draws from a range of disciplines and fields of study, with which the reader may only have a passing acquaintance. I approach information literacy from a constructionist perspective, which emphasizes the dialogic relationship between people and the meaning making that occurs through this relationship. I understand knowledge creation through social interaction, and focus on the way people construct meanings, understandings and identities in relation to the discourses and discursive activities through which their lives are lived. Consequently, my thinking about information literacy has an epistemological focus (e.g. *how we know what we know*), and I would argue that to focus only on the skills side of information literacy is to ignore the dialogical nature of interaction (i.e. talking, acting, thinking, valuing and believing).

In addition, the locus of my research has largely focused on non-academic or library settings, such as workplaces. In order to draw from the workplace, I have worked closely with novices who are commencing their training, and experts who have been engaged with practice for many years. This has been a useful approach because it has challenged the library-centred skills-based notion of information literacy and refocused attention towards the phenomenon as a socio-cultural practice and process.

This leads me to recast information literacy and define it in the following way. As a socio-cultural practice that facilitates:

> Knowledge of information sources within an environment and an understanding of how these sources and the activities used to access them is constructed through discourse. Information literacy is constituted through the connections that exist between people, artifacts, texts and bodily experiences that enable individuals to develop both subjective and intersubjective positions. Information literacy is a way of knowing the many environments that constitute an individual in the world. It is a catalyst that informs practice and is in turn informed by it.

From this perspective information literate people can be defined as 'People who have a deep awareness, connection, and fluency with the information environment. They are engaged, enabled, enriched and embodied by social, procedural and physical information.' (Lloyd, 2006, p. 578). As such, information-literate people:

- are informed about the socio-cultural and material traditions underpinning the foundations of their practice;
- have developed the practical information skills (technological and otherwise) to perform in their practice and understand the relationship between this experience and performance;
- recognize their bodily experiences as part of the information experience that informs practice;
- understand how information is used, disseminated and contested, and employs this information to inform practice; and,
- understand that information literacy is an ongoing process of development and change.

As you will have noticed, the definition of information literacy and the description of information literate people does not rely on describing the skill sets of information literate people, although they are an important element of information literacy practice. This is primarily because I understand information literacy to be a context-dependent practice, which over time enables a person to *know* their information landscapes and the range of information sources that are relevant for effective learning and practice. These sources are not only textual, but as we shall see can also be physical as well as social. The skills and attributes evident in information literate people will always be dependent on the context and discourse that shapes and prefigures these practices and activities within it.

If, as Bateson (1972, p. 454) suggests, 'information is any difference that makes a difference', then it seems reasonable to suggest that the *difference* will be determined by what is considered good information practice. What information is valued will also be determined by context and the social practices valued by those engaged in practice within that context. To unpack this definition further and to set the scene for the architecture of information literacy practice that will be presented later in the book, I make the following comments:

- As a *way of knowing* I suggest that information literacy facilitates knowing about:
  - how information is situated in a landscape;
  - what forms of information are valued;

- how to use information in order to achieve context-specific outcomes; and

- what information activities are appropriate and effective for information access.

■ By *engaged* I mean that information literate people:

- have the ability to locate information appropriate to their task;

- are able to evaluate information and make judgements about its appropriateness; and

- develop appropriate skills and competencies that will enable them to interrogate information from the range of information modalities available within the landscape.

■ By *enriched*, I mean being:

- subject to and understanding the transition that comes from information use (e.g. from novice to expert); and

- be able to think critically and reflexively about information.

■ By *enabled* I mean:

- having the ability to apply information;

- making links with information; and

- having the capacity to move beyond context and seeking information that will enhance practice.

■ By *empowered* I mean:

- understanding the nature of information literacy practice in relation to its reflective and reflexive power; and

- using that power to ensure that praxis (morally informed action) becomes part of everyday practice.

Therefore, I view information literacy as a complex and dynamic practice that is driven by context. When we view information literacy within educational contexts, one that emphasizes individual outcomes and embraces technology, the phenomenon may manifest itself as 'textual' or technological practice (Tuominen *et al.*, 2005, p. 337). Similarly in workplaces driven by technology, information literacy may be viewed as technological practice or computer literacy. In visually driven contexts, such as art or media studies, we may see information literacy practice and process, constituted through visual literacy. In situations that are driven by the oracy of culture, information literacy may be manifest as oral information or social practice. These scenarios should give you some idea that I also think that information literacy is complex and messy. Indeed it is my view that the more complex the information landscape, the messier the practice becomes and the greater the problem of being able to adequately describe and untangle the characteristics of information literacy! The reason for this is that information literacy is not always an explicit practice and is, therefore, not completely visible to outsiders who wish to research and understand it.

Theorizing information literacy as a meta-practice

Information literacy is a social practice that facilitates knowing about the information landscapes within which a person is situated. As with many phenomena this practice cannot be described adequately as a context-independent entity, it needs to be situated within a context for us to understand its nature and shape, how it is made manifest, how it is experienced, and how it is 'played out' between people interacting within an environment. Because it occurs within a setting, this phenomenon is subject to the social values and processes that structure a setting and influences the organization and execution of practice.

This leads me to make the following statements about information literacy that will set the scene for an information literacy architecture that will be presented in a later chapter.

Given my understanding of information:

- information literacy occurs within all contexts and acts as a catalyst for learning about context, its practices and processes;

- information literacy is constructed through the whole person engaging with the context. Therefore, information literacy will have epistemic, social and corporeal dimensions with varying emphases;

- the way in which information literacy manifests itself as practice and process will be influenced by the narrative of the landscape and its interpretation within context (i.e. information literacy is a socio-cultural practice) that will differ from one knowledge domain to another (e.g. it is a situated practice);

- the socio-cultural concerns of context will influence the privileging of certain practices over others; and

- the outcomes of information literacy vary according to the socio-cultural outcomes and expectations of the landscape's discourse. In some landscapes information literacy will result in a subjective position (e.g. information literacy is individualistic), while in others an intersubjective one will be evoked. In any landscape these outcomes are not mutually exclusive.

Conclusions

Social and practice theory open up new ways of seeing the phenomenon of information literacy as a practice that acts as a catalyst for formal and informal leaning. These theories provide a framework through which we can explore various landscapes to understand how information literacy facilitates not only knowing about the sources of information, but how, in the process of becoming information literate, people undergo a transformation from novice to expert. In addition, practice theories enable us to identify how socio-cultural processes furnish opportunities to engage with tacit and embodied forms of information, to determine how these processes influence the development of information-related behaviours and attributes. In Chapter 3 the various landscapes of information literacy will be explored and characterized.

References

Bateson, G. (1972). *Steps to an ecology of the mind*. San Francisco, CA: Jason Aronson Inc.

Bourdieu, P. (1984). *The logic of practice*. Cambridge: Polity Press.

Brown, J. and Duguid, P. (2001). Knowledge and organization: a social practice perspective. *Organization Science*, 12(2), 198–213.

Brown, J., Collins, A. and Duguid, P. (1989). Situated cognition and the culture of learning. *Educational Researcher*, 18, 32–42.

Buckland, M. (1991). Information as thing. *Journal of the American Society for Information Science*, 42, 351–360.

Case, D. (2007). *Looking for information: a survey of research on information seeking, needs and behaviour*. London: Academic Press.

Cheuk, B. (2002). Exploring information literacy in the workplace: a process approach. In C. Bruce and Candy. P. (Eds), *Information literacy around the world: advances in programs and research* (pp. 177–191). Wagga Wagga, NSW: Centre for Information Studies.

Choo, C.-W. (2007). Information seeking in organizations: epistemic contexts, and contests. *Information Research*, 12((2), Paper 298. Retrieved 4 November 2008 from http://InformationR.net/ir/12-2/paper298.html/.

Cornelius, I. (2004). Information and its philosophy. *Library Trends*, 52(3), 377–386.

Csordas, T. (1994). Embodiment and experience: The existential ground of body and self. Cambridge: Cambridge University Press.

Davenport, T. and Prusak, L. (2000). *Working knowledge: how organizations manage what they know*. Boston, MA: Harvard Business School Press.

Dervin, B. (1976). Strategies for dealing with human information needs: information or communication? *Journal of Broadcasting*, 20(3), 324–351.

Dewey, J. (1938). *Experience of education*. New York: Macmillan.

Dreyfus, H. (1991). *Being-in-the-world: a commentary of Heidegger's being and time division one*. Cambridge MA: MIT Press.

Elmborg, J. (2006). Critical information literacy: implications for instructional practice. *Journal of Academic Librarianship*, 32(2), 192–199.

Gee, J. P. (2000). New people in new worlds. In B. Cope and M. Kalantzis (Eds), *Multiliteracies: literacy learning and the design of social futures* (pp. 43–48). London: Routledge.

Giddens, A. (1984). *Constitution of society: outline of a theory of structuration*. Cambridge: Polity Press.

Goffman, E. (1983). The interaction order. *American Sociological Review*, 48, 1–17.

Johannisson, J. and Sundin, O. (2007). Putting discourse to work: information practices and the professional project of nurses. *Library Quarterly*, 2(77), 199–218.

Kemmis, S. (2006). What is professional practice? In C. Kanes (Ed.), *Developing professional practice*. New York: Springer. Retrieved 6 November 2007 from http://www.csu.edu.au/research/ripple/docs/Kemmis%20Prof%20Practice%20Chapter%20060419_14.pdf/.

Lave, J. and Wenger, E. (1991). *Situated learning: legitimate peripheral participation*. New York: Cambridge University Press.

Lloyd, A. (2006) Information literacy landscapes: An emerging picture. *Journal of Documentation*, 62(5), 570–583.

McClelland, J., Dahlberg, K. and Phihal, J. (2002). Learning in the ivory tower: students embodied experience. *College Teaching*, 50(1), 4–8.

McKenzie, P. (2003). A model of information practices in accounts of everyday life information seeking. *Journal of Documentation*, 59(1), 19–40.

Merleau-Ponty, M. (1962). *Phenomenology of perception*. London: Routledge and Kegan Paul.

Reckwitz, A. (2002). Toward a theory of social practices: a development in cultural theorizing. *European Journal of Social Theory*, 5(2), 243–263.

Ruben, B. D. (1992). The communication-information relationship in system-theoretic perspective. *Journal of the American Society for Information Science*, 43, 15–27.

Savolainen, R. (2007). Information behaviour and information practice; reviewing the 'umbrella concepts' of information seeking studies. *Library Quarterly*, 77(2), 109–132.

Schatzki, T. (2001). Introduction: practice theory. In T. Schatzki, K. Knorr Cetina and E. von Savigny (Eds), *The practice turn in contemporary theory* (pp. 1–14). London: Routledge.

Schatzki, T. (2002). *The site of the social: a philosophical account of the constitution of social life and change*. Pennsylvania, PA: Pennsylvania University Press.

Schwandt, T. (2003). Three epistemological stances for qualitative inquiry: interpretivisim, hermeneutics and social constructionism. In *Handbook of Qualitative Research* (2nd ed., pp. 189–213). Thousand Oaks, CA: Sage Publications.

Searle, J. (2003). Developing literacy. In J. Stevenson (Ed.), *Developing Vocational Expertise* (pp. 51–80). Crows Nest, NSW: Allen and Unwin.

Talja, S. (1997). Constituting 'information' and 'user' as research objects: a theory of knowledge formations as alternative to the information man theory. 14–16 August, 1996. *Information seeking in context: Proceedings of an international conference on research in information needs, seeking and use in different contexts*, Tampere, Finland.

Talja, S. (2006). The domain analytic approach to scholars information practices. In K. E. Fisher, S. Erdelez and L. McKechnie (Eds), *Theories of information behaviour* (pp. 123–127). Medford, NJ: Information Today, Inc.

Talja, S. and Hansen, P. (2005). Information sharing. In A. Spink and C. Cole (Eds), *New directions in human information behaviour* (pp. 113–134). Berlin: Springer.

Tennant, M. (1999). Is learning transferable? In D. Boud and J. Garrick (Eds), *Understanding learning at work* (pp. 165–179). London: Routledge.

Tuominen, K., Savolainen, R. and Talja, S. (2005). Information literacy as a sociotechnical practice. *Library Quarterly*, 75(3), 329–345.

Warmsley, D. J. and Lewis, G. J. (1984). *Human geography: behavioural approaches*. Essex: Longman Inc.

Wenger, E. (1998). *Communities of practice; learning, meaning and identity*. Cambridge: Cambridge University Press.

Wittgenstein, L. (1958). *Philosophical investigations*. The German text, with a revised English translation/by Ludwig Wittgenstein; translated by G. E. M. Anscombe. New York: Macmillan.

3

Information literacy practice in academic libraries and the higher education landscape

Introduction

Information literacy has been the subject of intense interest in the educational library sector and a number of literature reviews have resulted. These reviews include: Bruce (2000) who explored the territories of information literacy; Bawden (2001) who considered the various approaches to information literacy; and more recently Corrall's (2007) examination of information literacy in the context of higher education. Rader (2002) has covered information literacy development from 1973 to 2002, while Johnson and Jent (2005) and Johnson *et al.* (2007) have explored the literature in relation to information literacy instruction. Hughes *et al.* (2005) updated the work of Bruce (2000), by examining the developments in Australian information literacy research and practice. Internationally, Virkus (2003) has explored information literacy from a European perspective. Given the extent of these reviews this chapter does not attempt to be in any way inclusive of all that has been written in this sector. Instead literature has been selected for this chapter to demonstrate the range of themes that appear to be representative of the current thinking and practice of information literacy in the higher education and academic library landscape.

The reviews noted above reveal that the conception of information literacy as it is practised in higher education and academic libraries is bounded within a landscape that has a clearly defined user population and is influenced by perceptions and tensions related to learning and teaching in educational environments. Within this sector, information literacy loosely falls into a number of landscapes (primary, secondary and tertiary education), each driven by their own specific discourses and practices. Discourses are defined as the 'social arena in which common understandings are manifest in language, social practices and structure' (Fletcher, 1999, p. 143). It is through discourse that rules, conventions, structures and statements about practice are regulated (Mills, 2003).

In general within the context of academic librarianship, the discourse of information literacy is centred on effective access and operationalization of information by the individual, and this has led to debates about what information literacy is and how it should be described and practised in this setting. In one camp there are advocates who conceptualize information literacy as a skills-based literacy, where information literacy is equated to the information skills required in the information search process. In the other camp information literacy is conceptualized as a complex phenomenon, which acts as a catalyst for learning. Most often this reflects the research and critical thinking processes, which are understood by academic librarians and educators. Similarly, debates also exist in the literature about how information literacy should be taught by either being embedded in subjects or as a stand-alone specialism.

In the earlier periods of information literacy education, teaching efforts were loosely focused on orientation and bibliographic instruction (the use of the library and its tools), and later on user education. Examples of this approach are still evident in the literature. In more recent times there has been increasing interest towards developing pedagogy that incorporates information literacy practices. This accounts for the complex features of the phenomenon and emphasizes critical features, such as reflective practice and critical thinking.

This distinction in conceptualizing information literacy arises from epistemological and methodological differences, which influence how information literacy is researched and therefore understood (e.g. behaviourist versus constructivist or quantitative versus qualitative research approaches). These variations in perspective have led to tensions between librarian practitioners who tend to adopt a library-centric approach to information literacy and focus on the development of effective searching skills, and researchers who focus on information literacy as part of the learning process.

In the 1980s and 1990s academic librarians saw the concept and research of information literacy as being invariably linked to a relationship with print. However, with the explosion of information on the Internet and an increase in digitized and 'born digital' information, the phenomenon is increasingly linked with digital literacy and other forms of information and communication technologies. The online delivery of education by many universities has provided librarians with a strategic opportunity to shift the debate about information literacy to a whole of institution level, promoting information literacy as a generic information competency and a necessary graduate outcome (Corrall, 2007, 2008).

In this sector information literacy is also associated with specific practices and tools, which shape how we understand it and how it is manifest as a practice. The focus of information literacy has largely been centred on instrumental or cognitive views of learning, which have historically been framed within a Cartesian approach to learning. In this approach the mind becomes the focus of learning and other forms of information access (e.g. body and oracy) are considered as relatively minor players in the information literacy process. This approach has contributed to the early cognitivist/behaviouralist models that often frame information literacy objectively in terms of access to knowledge (viewed as external and discoverable). It also contributed to the development of information competencies, skills and attributes that must be demonstrated by the individual, in order for them to be assessed as being information literate.

When we talk about information literacy in the education sector we often talk about the *development and application* of skills. Here we refer to the activities of information literacy, such as developing strategies to meet information needs through activities such as information seeking, selecting and evaluating information, and the ethical presentation of information in the process of learning in a formal educational framework (Lennox and Walker, 1992). We also talk about the attributes of an information literate person, which centre on awareness of information, sources and strategies for accessing and using information (Doyle, 1992). The result of this understanding of information literacy is reflected in the number of definitions that focus on describing it in relation to behaviour, and a range of standards and frameworks that aim to guide information literacy development in the education sector; see, for example, ALA (American Library Association), SCONUL (Society of College, National and University Libraries), ANZIIL (Australian and New Zealand Institute for Information Literacy) Standards.

Foundation studies of information literacy in the higher education sector

During the late 1980s and early 1990s information literacy began to emerge as a significant area of research interest in curriculum studies, education and library practice. Since then there has been a significant amount of empirical research relating to information literacy in this sector. In the 1990s a small number of foundation studies changed the way in which information literacy was understood, in addition to broadening our perspective of what information literacy is and what being information literate means. There also exists a plethora of smaller-scale studies and articles, some empirical but many anecdotal. Practitioners who are interested in championing information literacy in their libraries generally undertake these. They are also used to raise awareness of their professional abilities as information specialists and to champion the critical role of the library in educational practice and in lifelong learning.

The Delphi study conducted by Doyle (1992) aimed at seeking consensus among experts and scholars of information literacy whose thinking had influenced the discourse about information literacy up until the 1990s. As a result of this study, a consensual definition of information literacy as 'the ability to access, evaluate and use information from a variety of sources' (p. 2) was produced. In addition, a set of attributes were developed by Doyle (1992, p. 2) to characterize the concept. These attributes reflect the research process and included:

- the recognition of an information need and the need for complete information;
- the ability to formulate questions;
- recognition of potential sources of information;
- development of successful search strategies;
- ability to evaluate, organize and apply information;
- ability to integrate information into bodies of knowledge; and
- the ability to think critically and solve problems using information.

Doyle also linked information literacy to the concept of lifelong learning, by suggesting that the accomplishment of these skills empowered individuals to make informed choices throughout life.

Doyle's pioneering study has been used as an exemplar in the educational sector and illustrates a behaviourist approach to information literacy, whereby the attributes of an information literate person, were identified and considered as separate from the context. Becoming information literate in an education context is understood as a subjective process whereby the individual experiences information as objective and external. In particular, it underpinned the development of information literacy standards and frameworks such as ACRL (Association of College and Research Libraries, 2000) in the USA, ANZIIL (Australian and New Zealand Institute for Information Literacy) in Australia and New Zealand (Bundy, 2004), and SCONUL (Society of College, National and University Libraries, 1999) in the UK and Ireland. In this context, information literacy is viewed as a generic skill, which once taught, is transferable across sectors.

In 1988, Kuhlthau undertook a qualitative study on information seeking that employed a constructivist approach. This study moved the conception of information literacy away from the development of library-based skills towards conceiving information literacy in relation to learning. Kuhlthau adopted a 'user perspective' in her qualitative study on secondary students' experiences of information seeking, producing a model of the information search process, which illustrated how students learnt from a range of information sources (Kuhlthau, 2004, p. 163). Kuhlthau (2004) contributed to the emerging information literacy agenda with her description of information literacy as a way of learning from a variety of sources rather than as a discrete set of information skills. This is highlighted by Kuhlthau when she suggests that 'there is a serious deficit in the advice given in many programs ... Information skills instruction that forms the basis of many information literacy programs frequently skips over the critical stages of reflecting, constructing, and internalising to learn and understand for one's self' (p. 163). Over a number of years this model has been refined by Kuhlthau and sets out common behaviours and patterns that are experienced by users when they undertake the process of seeking information (Kuhlthau, 2006).

A significant shift occurred in our understanding of information literacy with the publication of the *Seven Faces of Information Literacy* (Bruce, 1997). For the library and education sector this pioneering study heralded a change in the way information literacy could be conceived. Bruce's phenomenographic study (1996a) examined conceptions of information literacy among higher education academics, librarians and other workers who interacted intensively with information in this sector. Phenomenography is a research approach employed predominantly in teaching and learning environments, which uses strategies and techniques to identify variation in complex learning experiences, such as those that come about when a student interacts with information. The phenomenographic study, which described seven conceptions of experiences with information literacy recasts the framework developed through Doyle's (1992) research, by moving away from a behaviourist model, to describing information literacy as varying conceptions of experiencing information (Bruce, 1996a, p. 16). The research by Bruce

(1996a) identified the subject–object relationships from which information use is conceptualized. Two key elements of information literacy as it is manifest in educational contexts were represented within each conception, these were information use and information technology. A third element was different in each conceptualization giving each of the seven faces an individual character (Bruce, 1996a).

In Bruce's (1996a) study, experiences of information (faces 1–4) are viewed as objective and external to the individual. These faces related to technology, information sources, information process (the solving of problems) and the information control conception. The knowledge construction conception (face 5) is viewed as subjective and focuses on information use as the object of reflection becomes internalized (Bruce, 1997, p. 115). Bruce also viewed information literacy as being transformational; however, the transformation did not occur to the individual, but to others with whom the individual interacts (face 6) and to information, which is transformed into knowledge.

In identifying the scope of her research, Bruce illustrates the earlier point, that how information literacy is viewed and the way in which it is understood will be directly related to the discourse and discursive practices of the specific setting. Bruce makes this point when she states that 'it cannot be assumed that the experiences of higher educators match those of the information users in other workplaces' (Bruce, 1999, p. 157). Bruce's study of information literacy has provided the catalyst for many other phenomenographic information literacy studies, particularly in the area of learning, e.g. Boon *et al.* (2007), Edwards (2006), Limberg (2000, 2004) and Lupton (2008).

The research of Kuhlthau, Doyle and Bruce has been influential in developing the research agenda within the information literacy field, by introducing and articulating the concept, describing the experience and connecting it to other well known activities such as the information seeking process. In the next section we will see how this research has been translated into definitions of information literacy.

Definitions and descriptions of information literacy in the educational sector

There are numerous definitions of information literacy (Doyle, 1992; Behrens, 1994; Bruce, 1996a; Webber and Johnston, 2000); however, two types appear to dominate the literature. These two highlight the tensions that exist between the various approaches to understanding the phenomenon. The first emphasizes information literacy from a library-centric approach clearly focusing on skills and abilities and reveals the applied and instrumental nature of information literacy as it is articulated, taught and practised within a formal learning context. The second type of definition of information literacy, which has been used more recently, tends to emphasize the learning experience created when an individual engages and uses information.

In higher education and library contexts, information literacy is also strongly connected with the tools of learning (i.e. library catalogues, print media and digital technology sources). Therefore, descriptions and definitions focus on the individual's ability to develop skills and competencies in the navigation of information through textual and technological forms. In this context the individual develops and demonstrates an awareness of information sources and information skills in the process of engaging with content. The most frequently used, cited and adapted definition in the literature, is drawn from the American Library Association (ALA) Presidential Committee on Information Literacy (1989, p. 1). This definition highlights a range of behaviours required of an information literate person: 'To be information literate, a person must be able to recognize when information is needed and have the ability to locate, evaluate and use effectively the needed information.'

The ALA definition characterizes an information literate person as one who is able to consciously identify the need for information after which they must have the ability to execute a range of skills. These include the ability to effectively use the required information to make judgements about information against the setting from which the need has arisen. This definition was the starting point for the development of standards and guidelines for information literacy (particularly in the school and higher education sector). However, other definitions of information literacy have focused more on articulating the features of the information experience and the learning that is produced when these information skills are applied effectively.

As described in the last section, it was the groundbreaking research of Bruce that extended the ALA functional definition of the behaviours of locating and managing information to include the outcomes of these behaviours. Focusing more on the intellectual capabilities, Bruce (1998, p. 25) suggests that: 'The ability to locate, manage and use information has been labelled "Information literacy". Today information literacy is recognized as making an important contribution to decision making, problem solving, independent learning, continuing professional development and research.' Bruce's research is centred around the way people experience information in the higher education sector, and variations on that experience. In the last 10 years Bruce (2000, p. 97) has made a strong link between the phenomenon and learning, recognizing that in an educational context, information literacy is an 'appreciation of the complex ways of interacting with information. It is a way of thinking and reasoning about aspects of subject matter'. The relational nature of this interaction may combine aspects of computer literacy, learning to learn and information competencies and skills, including searching, locating, evaluating, selecting and organizing information, with the user becoming aware of the different ways of experiencing the use of information (Bruce, 2004, p. 9).

Placing a focus on students' and academics' understanding of the complexity of the information experience, Johnston and Webber (2003) also understand information literacy as a combination of behaviours appropriate to a specific setting. They suggest that information literacy is: '... the adoption of appropriate information behaviour to obtain, through whatever channel of medium, information well fitted to information needs, together with critical awareness of the importance of wise and ethical use of information in society (Johnston and Webber, 2003, p. 336).

Finally, Lupton (2004) describes information literacy as a 'learning approach' (p. 89) and has focused on the learning elements of information literacy, connecting the phenomenon with higher-order thinking processes that facilitates learning throughout life. Lupton describes information literacy broadly as having the following components: '... library research skills and "IT literacy" but it is broader than these. Information literacy is not just about finding and presenting information, it is about higher order analysis, synthesis, critical thinking and problem solving. It involves seeking and using information for independent learning, lifelong learning, participative citizenship and social responsibility' (Lupton, 2004, cited in Lupton et al., 2004, p. 1).

While only four definitions are presented here, from the many variations that exist, present in each, are the most common features of information literacy as defined and described in the education/library sectors. These features are: the individual's ability to define, locate, access and manage information; to use and present information ethically; to employ effective information seeking skills and information behaviours; and to think about information critically.

Critiques of information literacy

The current approaches to information literacy in the educational landscape are not, however, without critics who suggest that these views promote a largely unproblematic and often narrow conception. Challenging both the 'positivist philosophy' and 'information problem solving' aspects of information literacy, Kapitzke (2003, p. 49) argues that current information literacy frameworks based on these concepts are 'incompatible with emergent concepts of knowledge and epistemology for digital and online environments', which underpin the multiliteracy approach and have gained currency in education. In advocating a more critical information literacy approach, Kapitzke argues that the current frameworks fail to problematize the notion of information, its production and reproduction and the underlying influences that lead to and influence its creation. Kapitzke (2003) suggests that current explications of information literacy fail to:

> ... emphasize processes inside individual's heads, a critical information literacy would analyse the social and political ideologies embedded within the economies of ideas and information. Information literacy, as a method of approaching textual work, is not autonomous and neutral; it intersects with variables of gender, age, socioeconomic status, ethnicity, religion, and geographic location to generate different learning outcomes in different classrooms and educational contexts (p. 49).

Further, Kapitzke (2003, pp. 50–51) suggests that by focusing only on the written word, the current information literacy approach is centred on a single mode of 'representation and meaning'. Also, this singularity does not account for the multimodal nature of information access through diverse ranges of sources beyond print (i.e. sounds, vision, gesture). According to Kapitzke, a broader approach and more critical approach to information literacy is required, one that can account for the multimodal range of information access and dissemination tools, and the new forms of literacy that are coupled to this tools. She suggests that: 'A multiliteracies framework ... recognises that meaning making has always been multimodal and increasingly multimediated. The concept of a multiplicity of literacies extends beyond the locus of textual semiosis beyond language and print to sound, visuals, gestures and space, thereby giving legitimacy to what were hitherto marginalised communications media and textualities ...'. (Kapitzke, 2003, pp. 50–51).

Drawing from empirical research in other sectors, I have (2003) argued that current educational conceptions of information literacy tend to reify the phenomenon and promote it in generic and functional terms that are inappropriate for other sectors, where the focus is not on individual practice but on collective practice. I suggested that the educational sector treats information literacy as a 'single and discrete operational competency rather than as a constellation of competencies that engage the synchronous and serial applications of a range of perceptual, cognitive and process skills that together constitute a way of knowing' (p. 88). In addition, the individual and textual focus of information literacy in the education sector, fails to take into account the social and physical experience of human interaction that frame the collaborative and embodied nature of the experience in workplace sectors (Lloyd, 2005).

When referring to the ACRL (2000) standard for information literacy, Harris (2008) notes that any discussion or recognition of community, including the notion of a learning community and community of practices as the location for information literacy learning and practice, has been removed in favour of individual learning. Harris (2008, p. 254) argues that:

> The ability to recognise and comprehend the values of communities, and apply those values in the creation, transmission, or receipt of information, is a core activity in the development of 'common knowledge' between community members. Setting the stages of lifelong learning and information literacy development requires populating the scene with the individuals and communities that will guide, inspire, and help construct the learning environment and experiences ahead.

Information literacy as practice in educational settings

In the higher education sector, conceptions of information literacy have been generated largely by qualitative research approaches. These qualitative frameworks are generally translated by librarians into instructional models related to developing and demonstrating a range of information skills and behaviours. In addition, attempts have been made to quantify or measure these skills (see Catts, 2000). Common themes presented in this landscape relate to practitioner understanding of information literacy as an individual competency and the need to develop information-related skills in students. However, the way forward in this respect is not clear-cut. There is debate among practitioners about the best way to deliver information literacy education/instruction (e.g. stand-alone classes, integration or embedding of information literacy into curriculum), the application of prescriptive standards and guidelines, and the best way to assess information literacy. Underlying this debate is the nature of library/faculty partnerships, and whether librarians are adequately prepared through their own professional education and, therefore, have the requisite pedagogical knowledge and teaching skills to work with faculty and to take on teaching roles. Johnston and Webber (2003) have identified problems with these current practices, and have taken an innovative position by advocating information literacy as a separate discipline, rather than integrating information literacy into a curriculum model.

In a set of longitudinal studies on information literacy in academic libraries in Canada, Julien (2005) identified that information literacy is firmly connected to instruction around research strategies, use of technology, critical evaluation of the quality and usefulness of information, maximizing students' ability to locate information and find various sources of information. This view seems characteristic of how the construct of information literacy is understood by practitioners worldwide. Overall, Julien found that instructional classes and one-to-one instruction to be the norm with undergraduates continuing to be the focus of instruction and orientation. The importance of this study, however, is that it shows that librarians recognized the need to improve methods of teaching that appears to underlie a greater self-reflection on the nature of pedagogical expertise.

As modern universities and their libraries continue to move towards the provision of more distance education services there is increasing application of e-strategies and a need to develop effective online programmes and resources. This reflects on the university library collections, which are more focused on an increasing number and range of databases, ebooks and web 2.0 technologies (e.g. podcasts, blogs and wikis), used in course delivery. Consequently, the library practitioner focus tends to be towards developing information literacy instruction programmes through web-based tutorials. Increased publishing output on this topic is apparent and will continue to be an important area of research, which according to Johnson and Jent (2005, p. 487), reflects the trend of students as 'more and more are accessing libraries via the internet only and the instruction community is working to respond to this growing demand'.

Where face-to-face classes exist, there will be an emphasis on understanding database searching and the application of reference type skills, such as evaluation of content and source. In this instance there is a focus on the librarian as teacher or part of faculty and a deep commitment to information literacy as a pedagogical practice. There exists an increasing emphasis on developing pedagogically influenced models that aim to incorporate information literacy with learning theory and practice (e.g. Queensland University of Technology Information literacy Framework, http://www.library.qut.edu.au/services/teaching/infolit/framework.jsp/). Encouraging this movement of librarians to become deeply reflective practitioners about their pedagogical praxis, Jacobs (2008, p. 256) argues that: 'If we are going to address the issues of librarians' roles within educational endeavours systemically, we, as a discipline, need to foster reflective, critical habits of mind regarding pedagogical praxis ...'.

Information literacy instruction

The best way to teach information literacy has been a 'hotly' contested area, with substantial literature dedicated to this particular aspect, in addition to the merits of standalone versus integrated or embedded programmes. The diversity of the literature in this area reflects the epistemological stance of the library educator and their conception of information literacy. For example, in the preface to the ANZIIL information literacy framework, Bundy (2004) describes four approaches to information literacy curriculum development and delivery (generic, parallel, integrated and embedded). This issue has also been addressed by several authors in an edited information literacy volume on pedagogy and instruction (Andretta, 2007).

Generally in the higher education sector, information literacy instruction is viewed as the process of facilitating students' connection with textual sources such as: databases, web-based resources, through information and communication technology and print literacy, blending knowledge of sources with a range of skills and/or competencies that will enable an individual to use information effectively in this setting. In this sector there is a plethora of 'how to do it' articles that focus on the relationships between librarians and students, and librarians as collaborators with teaching staff. In an annotated bibliography of library instruction and information literacy, Johnson and Jent (2005), list collaboration, integration or embedding of information literacy within disciplines (such as law and medicine) as major themes emanating from the tertiary education and school sectors.

In recent times, there appears to be a greater recognition by higher education librarians that information literacy models need to adopt more than the skills-based approach (see Bruce *et al.*, 2007). Such an approach is reflective of the library skills/reference process, which librarians understand well, whereby students are instructed in the basics of searching and evaluating sources. Wang (2007, p. 156) suggests that:

> The focus of information literacy teaching needs to move from specific skills to general, transferable critical thinking and lifelong learning skills. When teachers and librarians move their teaching focus, they need to rethink pedagogies in information literacy teaching. Learning theories and information literacy standards should be used as the foundation of all information literacy learning design and activities.

Wang (2007) argues that the discipline is best taught collaboratively with students learning as a 'community of learners', this concept stemming from socio-cultural learning theory. The approach goes beyond the student-centred learning to focus more on the social and cultural aspects of the student's broader experiences. When this approach to teaching and learning is employed:

> (Students) engage in the class activities, interact with others and solve problems or complete tasks, think and talk about their thinking, and explore answers to the problems or tasks. The teacher acts as a motivator to encourage divergent answers and develop student critical thinking. In this learning environment, students' independent and reflective thinking skills will be improved.
>
> Wang (2007, p. 150).

The interest in embedding information literacy into the curriculum is noted by Johnson *et al.* (2007). In their 2007 bibliography the authors contend that there are a 'number of articles demonstrating a depth of information literacy curriculum integration (or embedding) previously not seen' (2007, p. 585). Stubbings and Franklin (2007, p. 145) argue in favour of this approach suggesting that embedding of information literacy into the subject curriculum greatly increases the impact on and relevance to students when it is 'delivered at a time of need'.

While there is much debate about information literacy instruction methods, the effectiveness of the approaches has been questioned by Koufogiannakis and Wiebe (2006). In a quantitative meta-analysis of information literacy teaching methods, the authors concluded that no one teaching method was more effective than another was. The study sought to find evidence about information literacy instruction methods that 'may have a direct impact on the way academic librarians approach teaching information literacy to undergraduate students' (p. 20). It was concluded by the authors, that there was not 'enough evidence to determine which teaching method is best' and that the evidence base for 'cognitive outcomes is weak' (p. 21). This analysis produced three fairly self-evident points that may influence the nature of teaching practice (p. 19):

- computer-assisted instruction is as effective as traditional instruction;

- traditional instruction is more effective than no instruction; and,

- self-directed, independent learning is more effective than no instruction.

Assessing students' information literacy practice

Within academic library practitioner literature there is a strong thread relating to ideas about assessment and the development of criteria and measurement of information literacy. This interest reflects librarians' responses to the meta-narratives of their workplaces, where information literacy assessment becomes a mark of a librarian's worth within the wider institution. Educational discourse tends to view information and knowledge as objective and codifiable. This positivist approach to information within the education sector is reflected in the conceptualization of information literacy as an assessable skill and competency and the call for information literacy programmes to produce assessable outcomes. Arguably this may produce a less critical approach to information and underplay the important features of critical thinking and reflexivity in favour of a standardized approach, which favours information skills development. While this may appear harsh criticism, it is also acknowledged that this representation of information literacy as a set of skills and competencies with information appears to be representative of the current educational climate and practice, which requires measurement and quantifiable evidence of outcome.

Catts (2000, p. 271) has argued that the 'achievement of information literacy should be a demonstrated outcome, rather than an assumed benefit of the tertiary experience'. Focusing on the skill aspect of information literacy, Catts (p. 271) also argues that assessment is critical to demonstrate the worth of the concept to both students as consumers of education and to convince employers about the 'quality' of the education being provided. He suggests that 'if information literacy is to be accepted as a valid outcome of higher education then some means of assessment is required, ideally at the level of the individual learner, and across programs, and for institutions as a whole' (p. 272).

Over the past 10 years in the USA, there has been a burgeoning of publications on assessment (see, for example, Johnson and Jent, 2005). Lindauer (2004, p. 122) indicates that in the USA this focus is driven by:

1 higher education regional accrediting agencies, which have made student learning outcomes assessment much more important;

2. the *Information Literacy Competency Standards for Higher Education*, which have been widely endorsed and applied and have spawned many initiatives and local collaborations; and

3. ALA divisions, such as ACRL and AASL, along with the Association for Research Libraries (ARL), which have made information literacy and assessment of outcomes a priority.

In the USA, guidelines and frameworks encourage the practice of assessment (e.g. the publication of ACRL framework). In 2002 ACRL defined the characteristics of best practice information literacy programmes. Assessment forms one of four key research agenda items for ACRL Research and Scholarship Committee (2003a).

Assessment and evaluation are essential parts of documenting the effects of library instruction and information literacy programmes. Future research in the areas of assessment, evaluation, and transferability needs to address involvement from stakeholders other than librarians, and include an integration of discipline-based standards or model academic standards (ACRL, 2003b, section 4 para 1).

Some excellent suggestions for planning and conducting assessment are given by Lindauer (2004) who provides an assessment context beyond student learning outcomes (performance measures on tests, course-embedded assignments, programme portfolios, course grades, self-assessment, and surveys of attitudes about the learning environment). She then adds the learning environment (curriculum, co-curriculum learning opportunities and independent learning opportunities) and the components of the information literacy programme, composed of courses, workshops, reference desk encounters, instructional learning opportunities by appointment, and independent learning opportunities. In the USA there are several national level information literacy assessment projects, for example, SAILS (Standardized Assessment of Information Literacy Skills, http://www.projectsails.org), is an online test that aims to document students' information skills and to identify areas that need improvement.

In the UK, Johnston and Webber (2003) have stressed that assessment of information literacy is vital; however, their approach differs from standard assessment approaches. They suggest that the focus should not only be on the assessment of the skills associated with information literacy practice but also on the theoretical underpinnings of the concept itself.

The issue of assessments is fraught with tensions and there is some debate within the literature. In their work for UNESCO on information literacy indicators, Catts and Lau (2008) advise that while such an approach is possible and desirable it is important to recognize that acceptance and support of standards and benchmarks is not universal, which underlies an epistemological tension among information literacy researchers, scholars and practitioners about whether information literacy is measurable. This illustrates the dichotomy that exists within this field. Measurement models of information literacy focus on behaviourist traits that can be translated to competencies and skills. Conversely, constructivist approaches tend to focus on how information is experienced and the meaning (for the learner) that is derived from that experience.

Education for information literacy practitioners

With increased interest in information literacy within this sector, the question of effective information literacy education for librarians also arises. Lindauer (2004) reports that while much has been written about effective teaching of information literacy and the strategic importance of assessment, there is little attention paid to strategies for the development of this practice. This author argues that this may relate to the academic library community being uncertain about how well their own training equips them to teach information literacy.

Elmborg (2006) suggests that the changing nature of reference from individual enquiry to group enquiry has led to shifts in demands for the librarian as service provider to librarian as educator and facilitator. This shift will result in a need for library education to 'develop new guiding philosophies' (p. 192) in order to better equip frontline practitioners to be effective trainers. With expanded roles that include being part of the faculty staff 'participating in curriculum revision and instructional initiatives' (p. 192). The author reports that not only do librarians feel unprepared for these roles but also that librarian education must better address these new roles. Elmborg suggests that 'librarians and library educators can better engage the educational climate on campuses by defining academic librarianship through the scholarship of teaching and learning in general, and the scholarship of literacy in particular' (p. 193). The need for effective teaching and assessment strategies, which will enable librarians to take on more complex and demanding teaching roles, is also echoed by Stubbings and Frank (2007). They argue that in order to promote the information literacy and learning connection and to further enhance students' learning experiences, 'librarians need a set of teaching skills, to further substantiate the educational aspect of information literacy' (p. 157).

In order for practitioners to become more engaged with these new information literacy roles, Jacobs (2008, p. 260) considers it important that library and information studies courses cover not only:

> Sound instructional strategies and techniques are an important part of teaching but they must be informed by an understanding of pedagogical theory and grounded in an understanding of broader educative initiatives occurring on our campuses ... Like information literacy itself, the teaching of information literacy can never be 'mastered' since both are always in flux, always contextual, always in process, always evolving. (p. 257)

Collaborative practices: librarian and faculty relationships

The practice of collaboration continues to receive attention in the education landscape. Factors that enhance collaboration between librarians, faculty and teachers have been analysed by Ivey (2003) and

Leong (2006) with the latter identifying the 'What's in it for me' factor as the single most persuasive argument (p. 10) to use with teachers. Having a shared understanding of how 'information literacy is developed' and having the 'appropriate staffing resources to develop and deliver the programs' is seen as vital (Ivey 2003, p. 100).

Conditions that enhance collaboration were identified by Ivey (2003, p. 100) as 'positive working relationships and effective communication' strategies. Leong (2006, p. 10) supports this and suggests that:

- the busyness of teachers ensured that information literacy programmes had to be offered at the 'point of need';

- regular communication is difficult to schedule but it is vital for the establishment of ongoing relationships; and

- establishing relationships based on mutual goals, shared understandings and recognized competence for the task.

Specific skill sets that librarians need include teaching, negotiation and advocacy skills. Further knowledge of pedagogy and education 'speak' enable librarians to 'push the right buttons' in an educational environment (Stubbings and Franklin 2007, p. 157). Such skills and knowledge need to be developed in library schools. According to Stubbings and Franklin (2007) currently librarians are developing these skills through extra study, workshops and conferences, for example, the Chartered Institute of Library and Information Professionals teaching workshops in the UK.

At the University of Melbourne, Australia, information literacy library practices, staffing profiles, university policy and programmes were refocused to drive stronger information literacy outcomes. The proponents reported that: 'The 12 former Library members of LRS were given a clear mandate to seek opportunities to work with academics to embed information literacy into their courses and to build communities of information literacy practice' (Bridgland and Whitehead, 2005, p. 56). Based on the organizational approach that Melbourne University's information literacy project took at the time, the authors believed that there were important elements for the long-term sustainability that other institutions need to consider; these were: 'The institutional endorsement of information literacy and the creation of a group of information specialists whose key role is to work with academics on the embedding of information literacy are beneficial, but they cannot work unless connections are built between individuals: social capital is an important factor in success' (Bridgland and Whitehead, 2005, p. 58). Providing some more detail on the role of the information specialists, Bridgland and Whitehead envisioned that information specialists would be educators, providing support for learning and teaching. As such, they would have a strong educational background, coupled with sound knowledge of teaching methodology. Added to this, information literacy educators would be experts in the application and integration of information and communication technologies into the learning environment (Bridgland and Whitehead, 2005, p. 55).

Programmes and frameworks for information literacy education

Programmes and frameworks for information literacy education also populate the literature from the higher education sector. The literature provides examples and models that conceptualize information literacy as well as highlight effective and innovative practice.

The six frames for information literacy (Bruce *et al.*, 2007) have been developed as a conceptual model for understanding how different views of information literacy influence pedagogical approaches to learning and teaching. The authors argue that the theoretical perspective that influences the way learning and teaching are understood will affect the delivery of information literacy education. This in turn will effect the development of information literacy curriculum design. These authors emphasize that information literacy is not a 'theory of learning' (p. 37) but 'rather that peoples' approach to information literacy and information literacy education are informed by the views of teaching, learning and information literacy which they adopt either implicitly or explicitly in different contexts' (p. 37). Designed as a conceptual tool and intended to orient reflection on the varied ways of seeing, developing and delivering information literacy curriculum, the 'frames' are described by Bruce *et al.* (2007, pp. 40–42) as:

- *Content frame*: discipline focused and centred on what users should know about information literacy. Assessment will focus on quantifying restatement and recall.

- *Competency frame*: viewed as a behavioural framework, which focuses on staged learner competency. Assessment will focus on testing skills and abilities.

- *Learning to learn framework*: oriented through constructivist theory with a focus on constructing knowledge and reflecting and evaluating the information processes that facilitate that construction.

- *Personal relevance frame*: oriented towards experiential learning of information literacy. The authors suggest that assessment might include portfolio development and reflection.

- *Social impact frame*: oriented towards social reform and centred around how information literacy impacts on the significant problems faced by communities. Examples are offered (i.e. digital divide).

- *Relational frame*: focused towards awareness of information literacy or the 'phenomena associated with it'.

This final frame (the relational frame) connects the content, learning to learn and experiential frame together. Therefore, it demonstrates that 'students experience information literacy in a range of ways that are more or less complex and powerful' (p. 43) and learning is the ability to adopt the experience of this complexity (p. 43). Information literacy from this perspective is, therefore, not about information skill or information behaviour development but rather about ways of interacting and experiencing information. The six frames provides a balanced and powerful tool for analysing how information literacy is viewed contextually and how that view influences the manifestation of information literacy practice.

The idea that reflection is central in 'bringing about learning' is identified by Hughes *et al.* (2007, p. 60). These authors argue that there is great disparity between learner's digital competence and their critical use of information (p. 59). By focusing on specific aspects of learning—e.g. reviewing the literature (Bruce, 1996b), searching the Internet (Edwards and Bruce, 2002) and the use of online information (Hughes *et al.*, 2006, p. 80)—the authors propose a series of models that take into consideration the vast differences that occur in student learning and ability through cultural, linguistic and educational experiences and the need to foster reflective use of information. International students in Australia are particularly affected because of their cultural and linguistic challenges in adapting in foreign learning environments, 'Extensive personal use of online technologies and "net-saviness" often contrast with unreflective approaches to information use' (Hughes *et al.*, 2007, p. 59). These models were progressively built, and they: 'all combine principles of reflective practice, action research and IL in a framework that provides a sound theoretical base for fostering a critical approach to information use for learning' (Hughes *et al.*, 2007, p. 60).

An important feature of these models is that they do not focus on specific competencies that have been ascribed for information literacy within the educational sector. Instead, they aim to promote an approach to information literacy that focuses on the students' experience of information use and attempts to frame this experience in a way that is accessible to curriculum designers and teachers (Hughes *et al.*, 2007). However, if this is the claim, then further work will need to be undertaken to understand the social and embodied experiences that are increasingly being recognized as part of the learning process.

Information literacy standards and frameworks in higher education

The idea that information literacy practices and process can be standardized has been a significant feature of the higher education landscape for the last 20 years and links to the assessment agenda. Librarians, particularly in the higher education sector, who have been the traditional champions of information literacy, have been active in translating conceptions of information literacy drawn from a limited field of empirical research, into lists of competencies, skills, attributes and behaviours. As this landscape is characterized by the relationship between individuals, codified knowledge, and the significant use of technology, then information literacy is focused on engaging with learning about sources of information and developing skills considered 'transferable' into other settings (Lloyd, 2003). This translation of research into practice has led to the development of frameworks, guidelines and standards for information literacy within this context.

An outcome of the research conducted by Doyle (1992) and Bruce (1996a), both discussed earlier, was the recognition of the contribution that information literacy made to learning, and the 'assumed' importance of information literacy as a generic skill, one that would enable an individual to continue learning throughout life. This recognition was widely accepted by librarians, particularly those in the higher education sector. It has led to the development of information literacy standards or frameworks that attempt to systematize the behaviours and skills of information literacy in a way that enables them to become assessable just as all other parts of the formal curriculum are.

In the USA, the ACRL standard is widely recognized as the definitive standard and it has been adopted in other countries also. The ACRL Information Literacy Competency Standards for Higher Education define information literacy as a set of abilities requiring individuals to 'recognise when information is needed and have the ability to locate, evaluate, and use effectively the needed information' (ACRL, 2000). The framework is used for assessing information literacy by presenting a number of competencies, which can be used by librarians or academic staff as indicators for information literacy.

This approach to information literacy synthesizes key areas of desirable behaviour that mark an information literate student, i.e. the information literate individual is able to (ACRL 2000, p. 3):

- determine the extent of the information needed;
- access the needed information effectively and efficiently;
- evaluate information its sources critically;
- incorporate selected information into one's knowledge base;
- use information effectively to accomplish a specific purpose; and
- understand the economic, legal and social issues surrounding the use of information and access and use information ethically and legally.

To support the standards, ACRL produced *Characteristics of programs of information literacy that illustrate best practices* (2003a) for undergraduate information literacy programmes. This document claims to represent a meta-set of exemplary practices that characterize information literacy excellence. It was compiled using a web-based Delphi polling technique involving librarians, faculty and higher education administration. The key characteristics of a best practice programme can be categorized into two broad fields. These are (ACRL, 2003a):

(a) *Strategic*—which includes information literacy in mission statements, aims and objectives, sound planning at a library and organizational level, establishing strong institution wide incorporation of information literacy; and

(b) *Operational*—which relates to staff expertise, development and support for information literacy, pedagogy, articulation with the curriculum, collaboration internally and with faculty, advocacy and assessment.

However, despite the ACRL standards and guidelines being made widely available, Julien (2005, p. 311) reports a low uptake of their use in Canada and, furthermore, indicates that only 'a small proportion (16%) of US libraries were using some information literacy standards'. Further: '... the best practices promoted by that organization, which include a wide range of organizational, planning, pedagogic, and evaluation recommendations (are not widely used)' (Julien 2005, p. 310). In her longitudinal study of information literacy practices in Canadian libraries, Julien (2005) observed that parts of the ACRL standards were not being addressed in practice, and she indicated that: 'Surprisingly, a significant proportion of respondents believed that librarians had no responsibility to teach an understanding of some ethical, economic, and sociopolitical information issues, an attitude clearly at odds with the ACRL standards.' (p. 310).

In Australia, the most commonly used definition of information literacy is located within the Australian and New Zealand Information Literacy Framework. This definition was adopted and adapted from the US standards, initially by the Council of Australian University Librarians (2001) and later revised by ANZIIL (Australian and New Zealand Institute for Information Literacy) (Bundy, 2004). Information literacy is defined by these standards as the understanding and ability that enable an individual to 'recognise when information is needed and have the capacity to locate, evaluate, and use effectively the needed information' (p. 3). According to the ANZIIL standards information literate people 'know when they need information, and are then able to identify, locate, evaluate, organise, and effectively use the information to address and help resolve personal, job related, or broader social issues and problems' (p. 3).

The Australian and New Zealand framework, presents six core standards as the basis for information literacy acquisition, understanding and application by an individual (Bundy, 2004, p. 11). The information literate person:

- recognizes the need for information and determines the nature and extent of the information needed;
- finds needed information effectively and efficiently;
- critically evaluates information and the information seeking process;
- manages information collected or generated;
- applies previous and new information to construct new concepts or create new understandings; and
- uses information with understanding and acknowledges cultural, ethical, economic, legal, and social issues surrounding the use of information.

In the UK, the SCONUL (Society of College, National and University Libraries) Task force originally published the *Information skills* model (1999), which was reconceptualized in 2004 as the Seven Pillars of Information Literacy model. This model recognizes information literacy as a hierarchical and progressive practice, with library and IT skills as the basic skills and information literacy as the higher-level concept within the information skills model. Drawing on the models from Bruce (1996a) and the work of Doyle (1992), Seven Pillars are described within this framework in which at the level of expert information use (i.e. information literate) a student should demonstrate the ability to:

- recognize an information need;
- distinguish ways of addressing an information gap;
- construct strategies for locating information;
- locate and access information;
- compare and evaluate information;
- organize, apply and communicate; and
- synthesize and create new knowledge.

SCONUL (2004)

All three frameworks—ACRL, ANZIIL, SCONUL—share a number of common elements, e.g. the ability to access information, recognition of the need for information, evaluation of information, manipulation and presentation of information and the understanding of ethical practices involved with information (Boon *et al.*, 2007), and may be seen as focusing on the competency level of information literacy (e.g. the development of demonstrable and assessable areas of skill acquisition). While the frameworks share a number of common elements, they also differ in their approach to the student learning process. Andretta (2005) highlights the differences in the following way: 'The main difference (between the frameworks) rests on the emphasis placed by ANZIIL and ACRL on the recursive knowledge construction approach, which provides a coherent framework for learning. SCONUL's interpretation of the knowledge creation process is too linear to reflect fully the learner's experience as it is based on a sequential progression' (p. 53).

Irrespective of the framework adopted, Webber (2006) suggests that for information literacy to have maximum impact it must have resonance with the organization. Webber (p. 3) highlights this when she states that:

> In the end, though, the most important thing is that the information literacy framework or definition is one that will (in the end, after a lot of work!) be accepted by the university at every level. Sometimes this can mean using an existing framework, but

sometimes it may be that developing a framework for information literacy can be part of the process of getting your institution to 'buy in' to the idea of information literacy.

In relation to the ACRL standards and the Objectives for Information Literacy Instruction (ACRL, 2001), Harris (2008) warns against seeing these as definitive, or as indicators of knowledge about the broader aspects of information literacy. He suggests that:

> The desire to keep these goals and objectives lean and precise makes teaching and learning about information literacy development a more efficient, and hopefully assessable, project. We must remember that the deployment of these standards, objectives, and outcomes designed for the assessment of information literacy development is not the core of this learning but merely indicators of new skills and knowledge in applied situations. (p. 254)

Further, Jacobs (2008) suggests that information literacy standards and outcomes-based assessment need to be used judiciously, because if these are used as the only consideration then this ignores the 'complex situatedness of information literacy', and information literacy's 'tremendous potential for creative, critical and visionary thinking' (p. 258). An important aspect of information literacy educators practice is the ability to recognize, reflect and understand the nature of 'situatedness' as identified by Jacobs (2008) or an individual learner's community context and value systems as described by (Harris, 2008).

Generally, in the higher education sector, information literacy has been linked to developing an individual's competency with information, with little recognition of the influence of community on the shaping of discourse or discursive practices that underpin competencies that are valued. Harris (2008) makes this point when he draws attention to broader aspects of information literacy and the need to consider the role of community in creating and influencing information literacy practice. He argues that: 'The processes of creating, locating, evaluating, and using information in various forms do not happen in a vacuum, away from community contexts where meanings and values are in play' (p. 250).

An argument in support of information literacy within the educational sector is that it prepares people for learning throughout life. However, as Harris (2008) has illustrated part of preparation for learning throughout life is an ability to understand how information is valued and knowledge constructed within the landscapes that students will populate once they have left their preparatory institutions. This is an area of information literacy research that has been silenced within current frameworks that continue to focus on the individual rather than the collaborative aspects of information literacy practice.

Advocacy, strategy and lifelong learning

Advocacy and strategy are also important themes in the literature for this sector, not only in terms of promoting the importance of information literacy as a critical aspect of learning, but also in terms of promoting the worth and value of the library profession. In the past 30 years librarians have championed the cause of information literacy as a prerequisite for effective learning both in education and throughout life. By doing so they have also attempted to place themselves in a strategic position in relation to their universities, thus helping to ensure the relevance and survival of the university library (sometimes the first to face funding cuts) and improve their status by reinventing their role as educators.

Bundy (2003) argues for broader ownership of the information literacy agenda and calls for greater collaboration between large academic libraries, public libraries and other agencies. He suggests that there are two fundamental reasons for this. The first relates to the lifelong learning agenda for which information literacy claims to be a prerequisite. The second relates to the rapid exponential increase in information and knowledge available in the educational sector that result in the rapid 'obsolescence' of content within first-degree courses. This means that students are increasingly being required to develop knowledge about how to learn and develop skills that will enable them to find and evaluate and apply new information in order to keep up with rapidly changing information environments (p. 6) and to develop skills that will meet the demands of 'fast capitalism' once they enter the workforce. In this respect, Bundy echoes the views of Zurkowski (1974) who first coined the term information literacy as a way of describing the information skills that would be required of service workers in the information age.

Part of the advocacy agenda has been the recognition that lifelong learning is not only the responsibility of the higher education sector but that greater collaboration between libraries across the various landscapes is required in order to strengthen support. Recognizing this need Bundy (2003) argues that broad connections need to be made beyond the formal educational institutions:

> There is a need for all types of librarians to make greater connection with each other beyond the traditional resource sharing and consortia, with their mutual interest in fostering information literate and information enabled young people as the key connector. Universities and their libraries cannot achieve their full potential in isolation from the other formal sectors of education. Nor can they do so in isolation from the informal educational sectors such as public libraries, of which typically, worldwide, 35% of users are students (pp. 8–9).

The need to advocate for the inclusion of information literacy as a key feature of university curriculum has been a major focus for academic librarians. In her 2002 background paper for UNESCO, the US National Commission on Libraries and Information Science, and the National Forum on Information Literacy (cited in Bruce, 2004), Bruce lists the key factors to the implementing information literacy programmes as:

- establishing policy and guidelines at an international, national and institutional level, which highlight information literacy education as the catalyst for critical and self-directed learning;
- education and staff development of teachers, information specialists and managers to ensure understanding of the importance of information literacy in learner development; and
- developing partnerships between key personnel and promoting the value of information literacy to students, information specialists, IT specialists, curriculum designers, community organizations and teachers and the importance of collaboration that can enable the 'teaching-learning experiences that promote self-directed and critical lifelong learning' (Bruce, 2002, p. 16).

At an international level the importance of strong advocacy mechanisms to promote information literacy in education was left in no doubt in the Alexandria Proclamation (Garner, 2006). One strand of the Meeting of Experts in Alexandria was dedicated to this critical and foundation aspect of information literacy. This strand identified the critical aspects of information literacy to be a focus of advocacy; the key recommendations were that there should be:

- educator preparation and professional development;
- evidence-based decision making;
- active pedagogical practices;
- nourishing educational environments; and
- information literacy requirements in assessment and accreditation.

Garner (2006, p. 11)

Being strategic about information literacy

The need to be strategic in relation to information literacy in the higher education sector has also been a theme within the literature. In the UK, Corrall (2008) analysed information literacy strategy documents of 10 higher education libraries. The author found that while information literacy is often present in institutional teaching and learning strategies (p. 27), 'the concept of an institutional level strategy or strategic plan for information literacy is gaining currency, particularly in Australia and the US'.

Corrall (2007) identified a number of recurring themes in this study. All universities surveyed embedded information literacy into disciplinary activity, working collaboratively whereby:

- almost all university libraries planned to develop e-learning resources alongside traditional information literacy interventions, and
- most proposed the adoption of professional standards to improve consistency, with a number proposing the SCONUL Seven Pillars Model as a framework.

Significant findings from this study suggest that:

- many strategists aspire to reach out beyond their traditional student constituency to help academic and other staff;
- the broad nature of partnering is envisaged (in most cases with other academic and administrative services, as well as academic staff);
- information literacy market development has received less attention in the literature, but could be connected with a recent UK initiative to develop 'i-skills' among all tertiary education staff;
- all 10 institutions reflected the educational dimension of their information literacy activities in reference to information literacy learning outcomes; and

- five explicitly recognized the strategic importance of information literacy practitioners being given the opportunity to develop teaching skills and pedagogical knowledge.

Corrall (2008, pp. 34–35)

In an earlier study, Corrall (2007) aimed to establish the level and nature of commitment (strategic engagement) to information literacy in 114 universities in the UK as evidenced in their publicly available documents. Surprisingly in only 75 institutions was there evidence found of engagement in information literacy at a strategic level.

Emerging from the Corrall (2007) study was an evaluation tool for institutions to self-assess or use for benchmarking the level of strategic engagement of their institution. The results of her literature review indicated that practitioners are concerned at the lack of progress by institutions to strategically engage with information literacy.

> Key proponents have argued that the concept needs to be embedded in mission, vision, strategy and policy statements of both the library and the institution, especially those related to education. Professional associations and individuals have incorporated these points in defining characteristics representing best practice benchmarks of institutional commitment, adding graduate attribute statements to the strategic documents identified.
>
> Corrall (2007, para 20)

From this study the concepts with prominence in many institution's strategic and policy documents were 'library and information services, information management, learning and teaching, and student skills'. However, less developed were statements about 'graduate attributes, and research'. While there was little attention in the literature, Corrall (2007) argues that several 'important elements in this strategic framework to encourage holistic conceptions of information literacy' are 'human resources and knowledge transfer' (section 5 Discussion, para 13).

Other indicators of engagement (Corrall, 2007, para 70) were found to be:

- positioning (level in a hierarchy, prominence within a document, priority in a set of issues, collocation with other items);
- precision (specificity of goals, attention to detail, clarity of phrasing);
- penetration (extent of coverage, number of documents, linkage of strategies).

Conclusions: information literacy practice in the education landscape

As indicated earlier, this section is a broad sweep of the literature and is only intended to cover the prevailing themes within this sector. In the higher education landscape the practice of information literacy is situated, shaped, interpreted and constituted through a Western educational discourse that emphasizes and values individual achievement. The information experience within this landscape is intended to develop a non-personalized view of information, knowledge and skills. Like literacy and learning, the educational landscape is a contested ground for information literacy practice. In this landscape there are two views of information literacy, one that views information as objective and external to the user and focuses on the development and application of skills that allow an engagement with codified knowledge. In this view, information literacy is a skill that is measurable. The other perspective also views information as objective, but emphasizes the subjective and transformational nature of this experience (Bruce, 1996a). From this view the emphasis is not on skill development but on enabling students to understand the variations in experiencing information in a reflective and critical way. This is not to say that either view is wrong, rather that the educational view of information literacy is one way of understanding the conception and this illustrates the importance of understanding how context and discourse prefigure specific understandings.

Despite these differing accounts of information literacy for this landscape there are a number of common features. The most important of these is that information is understood within this sector as objective and internal to the user; this understanding of information drives how information literacy is practised within this context. Therefore, information literacy can be characterized as:

- centred on an individual's experience of information;
- focused on access to the codified knowledge represented through the written word (either print or digital) and accessed using tools that characterize these spaces;
- concerned with the production of an information literate identity that corresponds to the educational narrative;
- explicates information literacy through the student research process, using a range of information skills, the most important being identified as: defining, locating, accessing, evaluating and presenting information as indicative of being information literate';

- concerned with establishing a range of indicators or measures for information literacy; and
- an acceptance that information literacy skills are transferable and therefore generic—however, this view is often a received view with little empirical evidence to support or justify it.

In this setting, the information activities of librarians are focused around:

- information sharing with the institutional community through advocacy for information literacy—this advocacy has two dimensions:
  - the first being in the interest of the student and improving information practice;
  - the second focuses more closely on issues of librarian's status and expansion of roles outside the library.
- identifying ways to measure or at least prove the worth of information literacy education to the wider education community and then sharing this information among the information literacy instruction community;
- librarians' reflection on their own pedagogical knowledge and ways to develop this; and
- reflexivity about their teaching skills and ways to develop and improve their own experiences and the learning experiences of students.

References

American Library Association ALA (1989) Presidential Committee on Information Literacy: Final Report. Retrieved 10 December 2008 from http://www.ala.org/ala/mgrps/divs/acrl/publications/whitepapers/presidential.cfm/.

Andretta, S. (2005). *Information literacy: a practitioner's guide*. Oxford: Chandos Publishing.

Andretta, S. (2007). *Change and challenge; information literacy for the 21st century*. Blackwood, SA: Auslib Press.

Association of College and Research Libraries (2000). Information literacy competency standards for higher education. Retrieved 20 December 2008 from http://www.ala.org/ala/mgrps/divs/acrl/standards/standards.pdf/.

Association of College and Research Libraries (2001). Objectives for Information Literacy Instruction: a model statement for academic librarians. American Library Association. Retrieved 13 January 2009 from http://www.ala.org/ala/mgrps/divs/acrl/standards/objectivesinformation.cfm

Association of College and Research Libraries (ACRL) (2003a). Characteristics of programs of information literacy that illustrate best practice: A guideline. Retrieved 20 December 2008 from http://www.ala.org/ala/mgrps/divs/acrl/standards/characteristics.cfm/.

Association of College and Research Libraries (ACRL) Research and Scholarship Committee (2003b). Research Agenda for Library and Information Literacy. Section IV Assessment. Retrieved 13 January 2009 from http://www.ala.org/ala/mgrps/divs/acrl/about/sections/is/projpubs/researchagendalibrary.cfm#assessment/.

Bawden, D. (2001). Information and digital literacies: a review of concepts. *Journal of Documentation*, 57(2), 218–259.

Behrens, S. (1994). A conceptual analysis and historical overview of information literacy. *College and Research Libraries*, 55, 309–322.

Boon, S., Johnston, B. and Webber, S. (2007). A phenomenographic study of English faculty's conceptions of information literacy. *Journal of Documentation*, 63(2), 204–228.

Bridgland, A. and Whitehead, M. (2005). Information literacy in the 'E' environment: an approach for sustainability. *Journal of Academic Librarianship*, 31(1), 4–59.

Bruce, C. (1996a). *Information literacy: a phenomenography.* Unpublished PhD, Armidale, NSW: University of New England.

Bruce, C. (1996b). From neophyte to expert counting on reflection to facilitate complex conceptions of the literature review. In O. Zuber-Skerritt (Ed.), *Frameworks for postgraduate education.* Lismore: Southern Cross University Press.

Bruce, C. (1997). *The seven faces of information literacy.* Adelaide: Auslib Press.

Bruce, C. (1998). The phenomenon of information literacy. *Higher Education Research and Development*, 17(1), 25–43.

Bruce, C. (1999). Workplace experiences of information literacy. *International Journal of Information Management*, 19, 33–47.

Bruce, C. (2000). Information literacy research; dimensions of the emerging collective consciousness. *Australian Academic and Research Libraries*, 31(2), 91–109.

Bruce, C. S. (2002). Information literacy as a catalyst for educational change: a background paper. White Paper prepared for UNESCO, the US National Commission on Libraries and Information Science, and the National Forum on information Literacy, for use at the Information Literacy Meeting of Experts, Prague, The Czech Republic, July 2002.

(Retrieved November 26, 2005 from http://dlist.sir.arizona.edu/300/01/bruce-fullpaper.pdf/.

Bruce, C. (2004). Information literacy as a catalyst for educational change: a background paper. *Lifelong learning: whose responsibility and what is your contribution.* Proceedings of the 3rd International Lifelong learning conference, Yeppoon, Queensland, Australia, 13–16 June, Rockhampton, Central Queensland University Press, pp 8–19.

Bruce, C., Edwards, S. and Lupton, M. (2007). Six frames for information literacy education: a conceptual framework for interpreting the relationship between theory and practice. In S. Andretta (Ed.), *Change and challenge: Information literacy for the 21st century* (pp. 37–58). Blackwood, SA: Auslib Press.

Bundy, A. (2003). *Opportunity and accountability: information literacy and libraries in higher education.* Paper presented at the Tertiary Alliance Libraries Group information literacy seminar. University of Waikato, Hamilton, NZ, September 2003. Retrieved 28 September 2008 from http://www.library.unisa.edu.au/about/papers/opportunity-and-accountability.pdf/.

Bundy, A. (2004). *Australian and New Zealand Information Literacy Framework: principles, standards and practice* (2nd ed.). Adelaide: Australian and New Zealand Institute for Information Literacy.

Catts, R. (2000). Some issues in assessing information literacy. In C. Bruce and P. Candy (Eds), *Information literacy around the world; advances in programs and research* (pp. 271–283). Wagga Wagga, NSW: Centre for Information Studies.

Catts, R. and Lau, J. (2008). *UNESCO information for all programme (IFAP). Towards information literacy indicators.* France: UNESCO. Retrieved 14 October, 2008 from http://unesdoc.unesco.org/images/0015/001587/158723e.pdf/.

Corrall, S. M. (2007). Benchmarking strategic engagement with information literacy in higher education: Towards a working model [Electronic Version]. *Information Research*, 12. Retrieved 20 May 2008 from http://InformationR.net/ir/12-4/paper328.html/.

Corrall, S. M. (2008). Information literacy strategy development in higher education: an exploratory study. *International Journal of Information Management*, 28, 26–34.

Doyle, C. (1992). Outcomes measures for information literacy within the national education goals of 1990. Final report to the national forum on information literacy. Summary of findings, ED351 033. Syracuse, NY: Eric Clearinghouse on Information and Technology.

Edwards, S. (2006). *Panning for gold: information literacy and the net lenses model.* Blackwood, SA: Auslib Press.

Edwards, S. and Bruce, C. (2002) Reflective Internet searching: an action research model. *The Learning Organization*, 9(4), 180–188.

Elmborg, J. (2006). Critical information literacy: implications for instructional practice. *Journal of Academic Librarianship*, 32(2), 192–199.

Fletcher, J. (1999). *Disappearing acts: gender, power and relational practice at work*. Cambridge, MA: MIT Press.

Garner, S. D. (2006). *High-level colloquium in information literacy and lifelong learning*. Report of a meeting sponsored by the United Nations Educational, Scientific and Cultural Organisation (UNESCO), National Forum on Information Literacy (NFIL) and the International Federation of Library Associations and Institutions (IFLA). Bibliotheca Alexandrina. Alexandria, Egypt, November 6–9, 2005. Retrieved August 2008, from http://archive.ifla.org/III/wsis/High-Level-Colloquium.pdf/.

Harris, B. (2008). Communities as necessity in information literacy development: challenging the standards. *Journal of Academic Librarianship*, 34(3), 248–255.

Hughes, H., Middleton, M., Edwards, S., Bruce, C. and McAllister, L. (2005). Information literacy research in Australia 2000–2005. *Bulletin des Bibliotheques de France, Translated from French by Oristelle Bonnis Bulletin des Bibliotheques de France*, 50(6), 45–55. Retrieved 28 June 2008 from http://eprints.qut.edu.au/2832/

Hughes, H., Bruce, C. S. and Edwards, S. L. (2006) Fostering a reflective approach to online information use for learning. In D. Orr, F. Nouwens, C. Macpherson, R. E. Harreveld and P. A. Danaher (Eds), *Lifelong learning: partners, pathways and pedagogies*. Keynote and refereed papers from the 4th International lifelong learning conference, Yepoon, Queensland (pp. 143–150). Rockhampton: Central Queensland University Press.

Hughes, H., Bruce, C., Edwards, S. (2007). Models for reflection and learning: a culturally inclusive response to the information literacy imbalance. In S. Andretta (Ed.). *Change and challenge: information literacy for the 21st century* (pp. 59–84). Blackwood, SA: Auslib Press.

Ivey, R. (2003). Information literacy: How do librarians and academics work in partnership? *Australian Academic and Research Libraries*, 34(2), 100–113.

Jacobs, H. (2008). Information literacy and reflective pedagogical praxis. *Journal of Academic Librarianship*, 34(3), 248–255.

Johnson, A. and Jent, S. (2005). Library instruction and information literacy—2005. *Reference Services Review*, 35(1), 137–186.

Johnson, A. M., Jent, S. and Reynolds, L. (2007). Library instruction and information literacy 2006. *Reference Services Review*, 35(4), 548–640.

Johnston, B. and Webber, S. (2003). Information literacy in higher education: a review and case study. *Studies in Higher Education,* 28(3).

Julien, H. (2005). A longitudinal analysis of information literacy instruction in Canadian academic libraries. *Canadian Journal of Information and Library Science*, 29(3), 289–313.

Kapitzke, S. (2003). Information literacy: a positivist epistemology and politics of outformation. *Educational Theory*, 53(1), 37–53.

Koufogiannakis, D. and Weibe, N. (2006). Effective methods for teaching information literacy skills to undergraduate students: a systematic review and meta-analysis. *Evidence Based Library and Information Practice*, 1(3), 3–43.

Kuhlthau, C. (2004). *Seeking meaning; a process approach to library and information science services* (2nd ed.). Westport, CT: Libraries Unlimited.

Kuhlthau, C. (2006). Kuhltahu's information search process. In K. E. Fisher, S. Erdelez and McKechnie (Eds), *Theories of information behaviour* (pp. 230–234). Medford, NJ: Information Today Inc.

Lave, J. and Wenger, E. (1991). *Situated learning: legitimate peripheral participation*. New York: Cambridge University Press.

Lennox, M. and Walker, M. (1992). Information literacy: challenge for the future. *International Journal for Information Literacy Research*, 4, 1–18.

Leong, K. (2006). *Information literacy and TAFE: challenging librarian and teacher collaboration in the VET sector in a TAFE Institute.* Paper presented at the 9th AVETRA Conference 2006, Global VET: Challenges at the global, national and local levels, University of Wollongong, 19–21 April 2006 retrieved 13 September 2008.

Limberg, L. (2000). Is there a relationship between information seeking and learning outcomes? In C. Bruce and P. Candy (Eds), *Information literacy around the world: advances in programs and research* (pp. 193–208). Wagga Wagga, NSW: Centre for Information Studies, Charles Sturt University.

Lindauer, B. (2004). The three arenas of information literacy assessment. *Reference and Users Services Quarterly*, 44(2), 122–129.

Lloyd, A. (2003). Information literacy: the metacompetency of the knowledge economy; an exploratory paper. *Journal of Librarianship and Information Science*, 35(2), 87–92.

Lloyd, A. (2005). Information literacy: different contexts, different concepts, different truths? *Journal of Librarianship and Information Science*, 37(2), 82–88.

Lupton, M. (2004). *The learning connection: information literacy and the student experience*. Blackwood, SA: Auslib Press.

Lupton, M. (2008). *Information literacy and learning.* Unpublished PhD, Queensland University of Technology.

Lupton, M., Glanville, C., McDonald, P. and Selzer, D. (2004) *Information literacy toolkit.* Brisbane: Griffith University. Retrieved January 2009 from http://www.griffith.edu.au/centre/gihe/griffith_graduate/toolkit/infoLit/InfoLitToolkit.pdf/.

Mills, S. (2003). *Michel Foucault.* London: Routledge.

Rader, H. (2002). Information literacy 1973–2002: a selected literature review. *Library Trends,* 51(2), 242–261.

SCONUL (1999). *Information skills in higher education: A SCONUL position paper,* Society of College, National and University Libraries, retrieved 20 December 2007 from http://www.sconul.ac.uk/groups/information_literacy/papers/Seven_pillars.html/.

SCONUL (2004). Society of College, National and University Libraries. *The seven pillars of information literacy model.* Retrieved from http://www.sconul.ac.uk/groups/information_literacy/sp/model.html/.

Stubbings, R. and Franklin, G. (2007). Does advocacy help to embed information literacy into the curriculum? A case study. In S. Andretta (Ed.), *Change and challenge: information literacy for the 21st century.* Adelaide: Auslib Press.

UNESCO, and IFLA. (2007). *Information literacy: an international state of the art report.* Retrieved 28 September 2007 http://portal.unesco.org/ci/en/ev.php-URL_ID=25262&URL_DO=DO_TOPIC&URL_SECTION=201.html/.

Virkus, S. (2003). Information literacy in Europe: a literature review. *Information Research,* 8(4), 1–102.

Wang, L. (2007). Sociocultural learning theories and information literacy teaching activities in higher education. *Reference and User Services Quarterly,* Winter(47), 2.

Webber, S. (2006). Information literacy in higher education. In K. Stopar and Z. Rabzeljl (Eds) *Informacijska Pismenost med teorijo in prakso: vloga visokošolskih in specialnih knji nic: Zbornik prispevkov.* [Information literacy between theory and practice: the role of academic and special libraries: Proceedings.] Ljubljana: ZBDS. pp. 9–20.

Webber, S. and Johnston, B. (2000). Conceptions of information literacy; new perspectives and implications. *Journal of Information Science,* 26(6), 381–397.

Zurkowski, P. (1974). *The information service environment: relationships and priorities.* National Commission on Libraries and Information Science, Washington DC, ERIC Clearinghouse on Information Resources, ED 100391.

4

Information literacy in the workplace landscape

Introduction

While there has been substantial research and advocacy for information literacy in the higher education sector, the origins lie in the workplace. The term information literacy is attributed to Zurkowski (1974, p. 178) who was concerned about the private service sector and its ability to cope with the emerging complexity of the information age. Zurkowski linked information literacy in this sector with the attainment of economic and workplace goals and the ability to solve problems around workplace tasks (Lloyd and Williamson, 2008).

Outside the educational landscape few attempts have been made to construct models or frameworks that: (1) conceptualize the practice and activities of information literacy; (2) give meaning to the experience of information literacy in other settings; (3) investigate the role and effect that the collaborative nature of workplaces has on the development of information literacy practice or outcomes; or (4) consider the implications of these issues in relation to the preparation of students for learning in the workplace. One reason for this is that the education sector has a specific focus on learning and teaching, centred on a concentrated cohort and on an information landscape that is characterized by formal learning through the systematic use of text and technologies. In contrast, workplaces and workplace interests are incredibly diverse, complex and messy. Learning about the requirements and practices of work occurs at both formal and informal levels and requires access to both explicit and tacit sources of information. Information literacy may not follow the systematic research-based process that is advocated by the higher education setting.

Locations for information literacy workplace research tend to focus around training, service and administrative sectors, where the focus is the delivery of information literacy training via the library, corporate business or service sector. Work groups in this sector have been characterized as white-collar or knowledge workers. There has been little research conducted in more applied and less information and communication technology-dependent sectors in the workplace. Additionally, to date, there is little literature that relates to information literacy as it is experienced through collaborative practice (i.e. as part of the informal learning) that occurs within the workplace.

Generally, in this sector two approaches can be identified in workplace information literacy research to date. The first approach parallels the education sector's understandings of information literacy as a skills-based literacy, where information literacy is seen in terms of the individual achieving competence and appropriate behaviours in the development and execution of information skills. The second, more recent approach, adopts a sociological perspective that aims to theorize information literacy in a broader sense by exploring how the setting and its participants influence the development of information literacy practices and the outcomes that are produced. In this sense, information literacy is understood from a holistic perspective, where the focus is not on the individual but on the collaborative aspects of meaning making and information exchange, necessary for co-participatory work practice and the development of a shared understanding about work. Both perspectives are valid and make substantial contributions to understanding information literacy. This illustrates the idea that context matters and will affect the way in which information literacy is practised and understood by participants and those who research the area. It also suggests that while researchers will try to give meaning to information literacy as a phenomenon, practitioners will attempt to view the same phenomenon from an operational standpoint.

In early reporting of workplace information literacy, writers tended to draw from the library and/or educational literature to extrapolate a skills-based approach (Burnheim, 1992) or conceptualization (Bruce, 1996). This led to librarians in this sector advocating information literacy as a generic skills-based competency without attending to questions of transfer or context. This understanding of information literacy has begun to be questioned, particularly when viewed in the context of transfer studies and workplace learning research. These studies have produced complex understandings of how workplace learning occurs and the efficacy of transfer from one context to another. Mutch (2000) argues that information use in higher education is bounded, contextualized and directed. This use differs in comparison with the workplace 'where their problems are messy and open-ended' (Mutch, 2000, p. 153). In my studies I have also questioned the legitimacy of transferring educational conceptions of information literacy directly into workplace learning, which has its own unique discourses and practices (Lloyd, 2003; Lloyd-Zantiotis 2004). More recently, the question has also been raised by Boon *et al.* (2007), who studied academic English faculty conceptions of information in the UK. These authors suggest that it is still 'librarians conceptions and experiences that have dominated the literature and their frameworks and models for information that have been most visible' (p. 205).

When researching workplace information literacy the majority of researchers have focused their efforts on skills, transfer of information literacy skills from education to workplace, workplace information use, and information seeking behaviour. While the reporting of empirical research in this sector is still emerging, it has become evident that generalizations from research in the educational sector to workplace situations do not necessarily reflect the realities of experience and use of information in those contexts. Nor does the research provide a clear understanding of the outcomes of information literacy practice. This is largely due to the varied nature of work and work practices where there are differing emphases on the types of learning that occur. There are also varying views on what constitutes information and knowledge, and on what processes and practices are considered legitimate. In workplaces with tertiary-trained workforces, information literacy is often understood and will be closely connected to skills with text and information and communication technologies. In those trained in the vocational education sector, information literacy is often connected with acquiring competency or employability skills and focuses around engaging with text, people and technology. The majority of studies that have been undertaken share a common focus on the individual's information experience, rather than on the how that experience is bounded through collective practice.

Foundation research into workplace information literacy

A number of major studies have been undertaken that explore information literacy (or information skills) in the workplace. Studies by Bruce (1996) and Cheuk (1998) focus primarily on the tertiary education sectors and tertiary-trained professionals, while a third (Lloyd-Zantiotis, 2004) focuses on the vocational and trained paraprofessional sector. It is interesting to note that while information and communication technology play a role in the first two studies, it is almost absent in this third study. This leads to questions about the importance of context in giving shape to information literacy, an issue that we will return to in a later chapter.

Bruce

Bruce's (1997) phenomenographic doctoral research, while being reported mainly in relation to the higher education sector (see Chapter 3), drew on the experiences of effective information use among knowledge workers such as librarians and IT professionals, academics, and staff in the higher education workplace. The outcomes of this published research known as the *Seven Faces of Information Literacy* identified seven different ways of experiencing information, which Bruce then extrapolated into the experience of information literacy in an educational workplace. According to Bruce (1999, p. 35), knowledge workers experienced information literacy in their workplaces as:

- varying emphases on technology;
- emphasis on the capacity to engage in broad professional responsibilities, rather than specific skills;
- social collaboration or interdependence between colleagues, rather than an emphasis on individual capability;
- need for the partnership of information intermediaries; and
- emphasis on intellectual manipulation of information rather than technical skill with IT.

Bruce's (1999, p. 46) conception of information literacy focuses on 'peoples' ability to operate effectively in an information society'. This author suggests that learning organizations should require their employees to possess a suite of information-based abilities in order to operate effectively. She lists this suite as: critical thinking, the ability to identify an information need, awareness of personal and professional ethics, and, the ability to evaluate and organize information and to use information effectively in problem solving. Bruce (1999) suggests these experiences should influence how information literacy is taught in professional education programmes. She warns against decontextualizing information literacy skills, arguing that they will have a 'short shelf life' and will fail the individual in the workplace unless they are learned in the context of workplace competencies and expectations.

Cheuk

The picture of workplace information use developed by Cheuk (1998) focused specifically on an activity of information literacy within a professional context, i.e. the information seeking and use processes of auditors. Working from a user-centred perspective, Cheuk (1998) identified that the information seeking process was largely individualistic and often unpredictable. The outcome of this research was a two-stage model described by Cheuk as information consumption and information supply. Cheuk's research contrasts with the systemic and prescriptive skills-based approach identified in the library literature, in that it illustrates that the information-seeking process and experience within the workplace may be viewed as an unstructured, cyclical and repetitive process of information seeking. In this research Cheuk claims a constructivist perspective, and employs a qualitative method of sense making derived from Dervin (1992) to develop a model of information literacy for internal auditors.

Cheuk (2000, p. 178) defined information literacy as 'going through an information seeking and use process to acquire new meaning and understanding'. This definition was extended by her for workplace contexts as 'a set of abilities for employees to recognize when information is needed and to locate, evaluate, organize and use information effectively, as well as the abilities to create, package and present information effectively to the intended audience' (Cheuk, 2002, intro, para 1). Cheuk's research has illustrated common information-seeking and use processes within the workplace that share similarities with educational conceptions of information literacy as a skills-based literacy. These include the need to plan the processes of seeking information, gathering of information (information consumption) and presentation of information (information supply). This study emphasized the diverse activities that characterize information seeking, and use processes in the 'real life practice in handling information at work' (2000, p. 183). These were described by Cheuk (2000, pp. 183–184) as follows:

- information seeking is not always necessary;
- information seeking is by trial and error;

- getting information is not equal to getting the answer;
- information seeking is not linear;
- information seeking is not a one-man job; and
- information relevance criteria change.

Cheuk's research also raises questions relating to whether alternative models of information literacy are required for the workplace. In particular, the assertion that information seeking is not always necessary, nor is it an individual activity, has been supported in other recent studies (Lloyd-Zantiotis, 2004; Hepworth and Smith, 2008). This view appears contrary to the understanding that prevails in the higher education sector that to be information literate a person must recognize that they need information and have developed the ability to find information.

While Bruce and Cheuk focused their research efforts on knowledge workers or workers employed in the higher education sector, I have shifted away from these sectors and grounded my research in vocational and paraprofessional settings. My work explores the nature and manifestation of information literacy as a collaborative practice in settings where the focus is primarily on informal learning related to the performance and practice of work.

Lloyd

My doctoral research (Lloyd-Zantiotis, 2004) and more recent work within the emergency services sector (Lloyd, 2007), has focused on workers who could not be classified as knowledge workers. The results from my study reveal another side to information literacy as a socio-cultural practice, one that informs learning about workplace practice and is in turn informed by it. A practice where the activity of sharing and interpreting information is just as important as the activities that enable access (Lloyd-Zantiotis, 2004). Drawing from socio-cultural and workplace learning theory, I recognize information literacy as a holistic practice, one where the focus is not on the individual's experience of information but on the individual's experience of information in *consort* with others. In fact, the way in which information literacy emerges as practice will be influenced by the discourse of the setting, which sanctions and legitimizes information modalities and information-related activities. Information literacy produces a way of knowing about the practices and processes that inform learning about context. This will be explored in more detail later in this chapter.

While the three large studies by Bruce, Cheuk and my own, briefly described above, have been influential in the illustration of information literacy in the workplace, other smaller studies have also been conducted that focus on the individual developing skills to use information. This view is similar to the prevailing education view of information literacy as a skills-based literacy or competency, one that is generic and transferable from one context to another.

Information literacy as a competency and skill

When first conceived by Zurkowski (1974), information literacy was associated with the ability to develop techniques and skills in the use of information tools that would assist with problem solving (Lloyd-Zantiotis, 2004). Zurkowski (1974, p. 6) stated that: 'People trained in the application of information sources to their work can be called information literate. They have learned techniques and skills for utilizing the wide range of information tools as well as primary sources in moulding information solutions to their problems.'

At the time of this description, the information age was dawning and Zurkowski recognized that computers would become an important feature of service work. Information literacy was viewed in functional terms, reflecting the functional view of reading and writing that prevailed in the 1970s. Zurkowski argued that those workers who were information literate, i.e. who had the ability to apply the techniques and skills and to interpret information to solve workplace problems would provide the competitive edge for business.

Parenthetically, the terms skill and competency are often used interchangeably in the library literature but they are in reality not the same things. A skill refers to a combination of abilities that are underpinned by specific knowledge and to 'a person's mental, manual, motor, perceptual or social abilities' (Tovey, 1997, p. 12). The standard at which the skill or task is performed can then be measured against an agreed set of performance or skill indicators (Tovey, 1997, p. 13). A competency is more than just a skill, it also addresses 'knowledge, skills and attitudes required of the individual to perform the job at the level required' (Tovey, 1997, p. 13). There are three aspects to competency (Tovey, 1997, p. 12), which:

- will include measurement against an independently agreed set of criteria;
- must be able to be demonstrated; and
- is a definition of satisfactory performance.

When information literacy is perceived as a competency with information, the focus turns towards the ability to create and apply a set of criteria that outlines a suite of skills, which can then be measured against performance. Information skills have been associated with those skills required to find, retrieve, analyse and use information. They are, in general, categorized as task definition skills, information seeking strategies, searching skills, the ability to synthesize and evaluate information (Webb and Powis, 2004).

This is best illustrated through the various standards for information literacy, which were described in the previous chapter (e.g. ACRL, ANZIIL, and SCONUL). However, it could be argued that this approach to understanding information literacy reflects a librarian's perspective of information literacy, which in many cases is focused on the context of education and individual learning rather than the context of work and the realities of collaborative workplace practice.

In Australia, information literacy was embraced in the vocational training sector by librarians who: (1) advocated for the development of skill and competency aspects of information literacy; (2) understood the empowering role of information literacy in building effective and efficient workplaces; and (3) saw information literacy education as a way of ensuring their relevance in this ever changing sector. However, a failure to clearly articulate the role of information literacy in relation to its contribution to workplace learning meant that the phenomenon received little attention by TAFE (Technical and Further Education) educators. While there was an initial flurry of activity around the promotion of information literacy in the 1980s and 1990s, this seems to have died down in the early years of the twenty-first century.

The idea that information skills are essential to workplace productivity has long been visible in the vocational education sector in Australia. While information literacy is not specifically mentioned, information competencies have been included in a range of reforms (e.g. reports by Finn, 1991; Mayer, 1992). Both reports emphasized the importance of students in this sector developing the capacity to collect, sift, and sort and analyse information. In the 1990s, Burnheim (1992) writing from this setting, advocated and described information literacy as a separate core competency, underpinned by a constellation of information-related skills, which enabled the individual to think critically about information. Burnheim connected information literacy with economic goals such as workplace efficiency and an ability to quickly adapt to change. A key characteristic of an information literate person according to this author was the ability to encompass change through the development of transferable skills. In this context, Burnheim also connected workplace information literacy to the lifelong learning agenda that was at the time emerging in the broader education sector. While arguing for information literacy as a core competency Burnheim (1992, p. 194) identified a list of goals that students who were studying through the vocational education sector should reach, which included:

- an awareness of the range of information resources available through a wide variety of information providers;
- a sound grounding in research process methods;
- a sound knowledge of how information and information resources are organized; and,
- students being confident, competent users of information resources.

A list of competencies were then described that needed to be mastered by students in order to achieve these goals. Burnheim suggested that these competencies need to be the core across all subjects rather than subject specific, highlighting his understanding of information literacy as a generic competency. These competencies were listed (p. 194) as the ability to:

- formulate and analyse the information need;
- identify and appraise the worth of likely sources;
- trace and locate individual resources;
- examine, select and reject individual resources in the light of the information need;
- interrogate resources to isolate required information;
- record and store information;
- interpret, analyse, synthesize and evaluate the information gathered;
- present and communicate findings; and
- evaluate the conduct of the process.

This understanding of information literacy was influenced by the earlier work that had been undertaken in the educational sector (e.g. Breivik, 1985) and was formed around an understanding of information as objective, discoverable and reproducible. In this view of information literacy emphasis was placed on the individual achieving a mastery of information and the skills required to access it.

The idea of information literacy as a core competency for workers, and one that is critical to building and maintaining organizational capacity, has been explored in Australia by Gasteen and O'Sullivan (2000) who connect information literacy to an organization's capacity to build and maintain knowledge. In their study of a legal firm, the development of information literacy is viewed as central to a lawyer's skills and a requirement of the workplace as a learning organization. Based on their study, Gasteen and O'Sullivan connect information literacy to the attainment, through training, of information skills such as the ability to define, locate, evaluate, manage and organize information. In addition to skills training, these authors suggest that to support employees in their work, librarians must develop the ability to scaffold their understanding of information literacy to concepts used in the workplace, to ensure that information literacy training is relevant. The authors (Gasteen and O'Sullivan, 2002, p. 13) suggest that: 'We must broaden our outlook, see ourselves as part of the business and pursue interests that are relevant to it. It involves changing the way we envisage our role. In a knowledge based world, no one can afford to live in an ivory tower'.

The authors conclude that librarians need to understand their practice in relation to information literacy in the workplace and consider adapting and embracing the language of the business world, aligning information literacy as an information or knowledge economy concept.

Smith and Martina (2004) advocate that information literacy is equally important in the vocational education sector; however, they note the assumption of their tertiary education counterparts, that there is not as much urgency in embedding information literacy into the vocational educational curriculum as most students are learning a trade. This reinforces Stevenson's (2002, p. 2) argument that historically, vocational and workplace knowledge has traditionally been relegated to 'second best' because it is primarily believed to be concerned with the 'material, the technical, and the routine'. In a small study, undertaken from a library-centric and skills-based perspective, Smith and Martina (2004), explored the baking industry in Australia, and focused their examination on the relationship between information literacy and 'employability' skills (previously known in Australia as key competencies), which described generic skills required by all employees. They (p. 329) concluded that:

> It is not enough to show students how to use a particular library or where to find the books they need. By definition, if the skill is taught and understood then it becomes an employable skill. Students will then be able to relate finding information to their everyday working environment and to their adult life in general.

In a snapshot of information literacy practices by TAFE librarians in Victoria, Australia, Fafeita (2005) identified a raft of issues that impact on the effective implementation of information literacy programmes. Issues that are familiar to librarians in higher education sector (Fafeita, 2005, p. 106), included:

- a lack of consensus about the term information literacy;
- a narrow conception of the practice that focuses on skills;
- the operational boundaries in which TAFE librarians are required to work, time constraints within the already packed vocational curriculum, which limits opportunities to effectively embed information literacy practice;
- lack of resources to support the development of information literacy programmes;
- users' attitudes towards learning about information literacy skills until the point when they need it;
- the barriers presented with language and PC skills of clients; and
- teachers' failure to understand the information literacy concept and how it could benefit students were also identified a barrier.

Many of the barriers point to the lack of research in the vocational education sector resulting in a failure to adequately conceptualize and articulate information literacy for practitioners and educators within this sector. The long-term impact is becoming increasingly evident in the literature that focuses on information literacy skill development and work ready employees.

Corporate and small business sectors

Rosenberg (2002) in the USA has explored the importance of information literacy as a necessary skill in the operation of small businesses, particularly in the global networked world. Rosenberg emphasized that employees in small business are often under-equipped in key information skills such as the ability to evaluate information found on the Internet. He argued that small business employees 'must understand the value of information and must be able to acquire and use information' (p. 8) and that this will require employees who have developed sophisticated information literacy practice. Rosenberg (2002, p. 10) states that:

> Successful business people have long known that having certain types of information conveys a significant strategic advantage to a company. Also new is the importance of information literacy in the new global marketplace. Information literacy was always important to businesses, but now it takes on a new importance because of the changes wrought by the new network technologies. When businesses are connected to each other, information becomes especially valuable.

The lack of information literacy skills of employees in SMEs (small to medium businesses), particularly web-based information, is evidenced in De Saulles (2007) who argues that UK government policy intervention is needed to optimize their major investment in information and communication technology infrastructure. Major policy and investment in information literacy training is needed to make SME employees information literate in business information. He argues that the cost of time wasting and inefficient information searching on the web, to UK SMEs, reached somewhere in the vicinity of £3.7–8.2 billion per year.

While De Saulles (2007) discusses SMEs, a report by Kielstra for the Economist Intelligence Unit on company decision making, expresses concern that executives and workers do not have the information to make critical business decisions. In this worldwide online survey and follow-up in-depth interviews of 154 business executives, a number of issues were identified that run to the core of the information literacy agenda. These highlight the need for stronger advocacy for the development of information literacy practice and skills in the workplace as one expert stated in this study 'you cannot make proper decisions without proper information' (Economist Intelligence Unit, 2007, p. 2). The results of this study indicate that there is concern among executives that in highly competitive markets the lack of information or poor information leads to poor decisions. In this respect there is recognition that information not only relates to codified knowledge (e.g. as financial data) but is also important when it relates to competitor knowledge, market environments and the company itself. The report also highlights the importance of collaborative practices, and it indicates that while technology helps to a point (p. 7) executives also value the importance of other people as a strategic information source as most decisions were made on an ad hoc or informal basis. While not discussed by the authors, this response alludes to the need to trust the information of other people and suggests that collaborative networks play an important part in decision making. The report by Kielstra (Economist Intelligence Unit, 2007, p. 14) concludes with two broad areas for future focus: 'The first is in obtaining, filtering and verifying the necessary data need for decision makers. This is where technology comes into play ... The other is to understand how human beings fit into the process.'

Understanding the strategic value of information literacy in the decision making cycle has been absent from the current research suite of studies into workplace information literacy. This area represents an important area for future study, which may then promote the importance of information literacy practice.

Adding to the weight of evidence that points to the costs involved in not having an information literate workforce, Breivik (2005) notes that, Don Cohen a Ford Motor Company executive describes that cost in terms of time: 'The costs of information illiteracy are high ... We typically can only find half of the information we need to do our jobs and spend up to 30 percent of our time looking for the other half' (Cohen 1998, p. 21 cited in Breivik 2005, p. 23). The cost is also recognized in the US Department of the Navy, where it is estimated that that average worker 'spends an estimated 150 hours per year looking for information' (Bennett, 2001, p. 1 cited in Breivik, 2005, p. 23). Breivik notes that the loss of time and productivity described by these authors could be greatly reduced by an information literate workforce (Breivik, 2005, p. 23).

The idea that good information literacy practice is expected by employers, although this expectation is assumed rather than made explicit, has been explored in Scotland by Irving and Crawford (2008). These authors advocate the need to develop an overarching framework of information literacy competencies and skills that can be recognized and understood in the education sector and can then be applied to the workplace. In advocating for a National Information Literacy Framework for Scotland, Irving and Crawford (2008, p. 7) draw from the SCONUL Seven Pillars Model developed for higher education in the UK. The framework involves several skills and competencies defined by the Chartered Institute of Library and Information Professionals (CILIP group) as requiring the individual to develop an understanding of:

- a need for information;
- the resources available;
- how to find information;
- the need to evaluate results;
- how to work with or exploit results;
- ethics and responsibility of use;
- how to communicate or share your findings; and
- how to manage your findings.

A more recent study by these authors on the use of information in the workplace and its role in decision making stated among its conclusions that, in Scottish workplaces (Crawford and Irving, 2009, p. 9),

- people must be recognized as a legitimate source of workplace information;
- information literacy must be highly targeted;
- skills audits are required before designing information literacy training programmes;
- there is widespread understanding of what constitutes information literacy, but this understanding is implicit rather than explicit.

Advocating information literacy skills into the workplace

While there is significant attention paid to developing information literacy and its value to students in the education sector, the question of how information literacy can be made explicit and implemented into formal workplace training has received little attention in the literature. This represents a gap that requires serious attention from researchers and practitioners.

Attempting to implement information literacy strategies into the workplace can be facilitated, in the view of Oman (2001) by taking an organization-wide implementation approach. This author suggests that when presenting the case to management, demonstrating the value of information literacy to the company is a key argument followed up with 'tactical solutions' for implementation. She argues that:

> Placing your initiative in the silo of your group will not work. Success is more likely when you tie information literacy to internal employee development and compensation plans. The reality is, the 'what's in it for me' factor is a much stronger incentive than any other benefit your group can describe. This needs to be explained to management, potential internal partners, and individual employees (para 20).

Oman also suggests that a further opportunity for information literacy development in an organization might reside in demonstrating the links between information literacy and knowledge management. This is a view shared by Cheuk (2002) and O'Sullivan (2002). Other opportunities identified by Oman (2001) and O'Sullivan (2002) were partnering with human resources to identify information literacy competencies and training needs, and the mapping of information literacy skills against business processes.

The notion that information literacy must be promoted in the workplace has been considered by a number of authors. In her report to UNESCO on information literacy in the corporate workplace, Cheuk (2002, p. 5) suggests that people are 'drowning in the sea of information' because they are not equipped with the necessary information literacy skills; a concern originally expressed by Zurkowski in 1974. At the same time, Cheuk reports that workplaces provide limited opportunities for information literacy training to occur because of the lack of awareness about information literacy in work settings (2002, p. 5). Cheuk recognizes a number of barriers that affect the promotion of information literacy in workplace settings. She lists these (p. 10) as the:

- lack of familiarity with the terminology related to the concept of information literacy;
- differing mindsets between the workplace and education settings, in particular, a change in corporate culture towards valuing innovative thinking and problem solving; and
- the expectation that employees come to the workplace with information literacy skills already established, which results in these skills not being promoted in the workplace.

Cheuk (2002, p. 9) identified a number of factors that could be used to promote information in the workplace. These are:

- training on optimizing new technologies that manage information;
- including information literacy into the curriculum of continuous education and training schemes;
- increasing employee awareness about the fact that they are knowledge workers that access and use information in their day to day work;
- recognizing information literacy as a critical business skill and equally as important as communication or presentation skills; and
- recognizing the achievements of employees who create quality information.

Barriers to effective promotion and advocacy of information literacy in the workplace have been recognized by a number of authors. These activities rest on the ability of librarians and researchers to translate and articulate the concept of information literacy in ways that can be understood by employers (O'Sullivan 2002; Hepworth and Smith 2008). While specifically addressing this issue in relation to corporate business O'Sullivan's (2002) words resonate as relevant to all workplace sectors when she suggest that: 'Language and communication is part of the problem as demonstrated by the exercise of searching for library jargon in business literature. Because library terminology is foreign to corporate managers, the first step is to apply corporate terminology to relevant information concepts ... So we must search for new ways of describing information literacy and align it with business concepts' (p. 13).

The predominant workplace information literacy themes in the literature reveal that for this sector there is a prevailing behaviourist/cognitivist view of information literacy, related to the individual attainment of information skills and attributes. These are largely focused around text and technology and uncoupled to the realities of workplace practice and performance. However, other views of information literacy are also emerging from this sector. Drawing largely from socio-cultural theory, which considers the information experience in a broader sense as related to developing intersubjective positions, which enable the development of workplace identity and co-participatory work practice. In this view, the focus is more holistic and considers the information relationships between people in situ, the importance of information sharing as a collaborative practice and the influence of discourse in shaping the information practices of the workplace.

Beyond skills

Moving beyond the information skills needed in the post-Fordist workplace, Kapitzke (2003) believes that information literacy as it is taught in classrooms needs to better prepare students with attributes necessary for the transitory nature of the global workplace. Here workers are required to be adaptable and flexible and to understand how knowledge is constructed, contested and socially distributed across networked workplaces. She suggests that:

> Industry today focuses on speed, flexibility, and innovation; expertise is viewed not as a product but as a fluid process. Knowledge is developed within globally spread communities of practice that are embodied in organizational, intellectual, social, cultural and material interactions among members with a range of tools and technologies. New workplaces have a greater need for people who are good at collaborating and sharing knowledge than for smart individuals who, when they leave the enterprise, take their skills and expertise with them (p. 48).

Hepworth and Smith (2008) compared the information literacy needs of non-academic staff employed in higher education with the JISC (Joint Information Systems Committee) i-skills model. The model identifies a number of elements in the information cycle (i.e. information need, assessment of need, information retrieval, critical evaluation, adaptation of information, organization communication and review of information) (p. 214). In discussing their findings, the authors noted that the workplace model of i-skills is 'very different from that in the academic context' (p. 226). Where 'common conceptions of information literacy describe the process a researcher or student follows in completing an individual task or assignment' (p. 226). They argue that ' ... i-skills, stemming from the academic context, rather than being a generic phenomena commonly understood by all, may be context specific and people's experience of information literacy may not echo LIS conceptions of information literacy' (p. 226). This statement supports my workplace research (2005a,b, 2006a,b) that argued that information literacy practice will manifest differently according to the context in which it is practised. I have also suggested that the standards and guidelines for information literacy that have been developed in educational contexts may not be appropriate for describing and understanding the information literacy practice in other settings (Lloyd, 2003).

In their study, Hepworth and Smith (2008) identified that employees often do not have to identify an information need, partly because managers assigned well-defined tasks. Interestingly, in my (2004, 2007) studies of emergency services workers it was also noted that the need to identify a topic or the identification of an information need was not recognized by novices. This was because tasks and the required information were provided by more experienced officers, who identified the need through observation of novice practice.

Hepworth and Smith also noted in their study that the information experience was collaborative and was manifest through teamwork rather than focused on individuals, pointing to social dimensions of the information literacy experience being important, a point I also raised in 2005. Hepworth and Smith (2008, p. 227) suggest that 'If librarians and information professionals wish to support information literacy in the work context, they need to take on board a wider conception of the information landscape and information management in the workplace. Plus they need to appreciate the socially embedded nature of information literacy'.

In their exploration of this cycle, Hepworth and Smith (2008) identified other skills not evident in the JISC cycle that had a 'significant bearing on staff management of information' (p. 220). These skills were related to issues (pp. 222–223), such as:

- time management and information overload, which require judgement skills;
- the need for social networking skills (internal and external to the institution) including; 'the ability to identify and connect with other people; and, ask precise and accurate questions in order to elicit the required information were significant and necessary skills'.
- listening and having the ability to sift through information and make judgements about relevancy were also considered important; and
- development of team-working skills, primarily because information expertise and skill is normally spread across a team rather than just located.

Information literacy from a socio-cultural perspective: Lloyd's workplace studies

In this next section two studies of workplace information literacy practice are described. My interest in workplace information literacy is to understand how information literacy is used as a socio-cultural practice in order to establish participants in the practice and performances of the workplace. The focus of these discourse-oriented studies was to understand the nature of information literacy and identify how it enables access to the social, cultural, material and technical ways of knowing the workplace landscape, in particular, how information literacy:

- manifests in the process of learning about sociality of the workplace as an intersubjective space; and

- enables the development of practical understandings about the performance of work.

In both studies, information literacy was identified as a holistic and situated experience, which I reconceptualized (2007) as a complex socio-cultural practice. This places emphasis not only on the information produced, but also on the way information is understood, interpreted, shared and sanctioned by members who are engaged in collective practice. In this way information literacy becomes a critical catalyst in the construction of meaningful frameworks about workplace practice, regardless of what that practice is.

Through my research (2003, 2005a,b 2006b) I have reconceptualized information literacy as a practice that facilitates a 'way of knowing' about the sources of information that will inform performance and participation. These information sources are not confined to textual sources but are also social and physical sources that constitute an information landscape, producing an information experience that has embodied and social dimensions in addition to the cognitive. Consequently, I understand information literacy as being holistic.

Exploring information literacy outside traditional classroom and library contexts, I understand workplace information literacy from a constructionist perspective, as a complex, messy and collaborative. By engaging in this practice, the member comes to know the information environment, in particular, the information modalities that are sanctioned as legitimate sources of knowledge and the information activities related to the specific setting in which they work.

My interest in information literacy lies in developing an understanding of how the whole body engages with an information landscape. I question whether the experience of information literacy in educational contexts (and the behaviours and skills learnt there) can effectively transfer from educational environments to workplaces given there are differing discourses (e.g. histories, assumptions, values and ways of relating) that influence what information and knowledge are authorized and the ways of participation that are encouraged. My contribution to information literacy lies in the richer understanding of the modalities of information within a landscape, in particular, the role that social and corporeal (body) modalities play as sources of information.

Based on my research information literacy is:

- an intersubjective accomplishment because workplaces emphasize the importance of teamwork and collaboration:
  - this requires workplace participants to develop a shared view of practice and profession and a shared understanding of information;
  - it necessitates engaging with information that is valued by the community of workers;
- dependent upon the opportunities (affordances) offered to newcomers by experienced practitioners within the community of practice;
- a transformative process, in which the new worker's engagement with information facilitates over time the transition of workplace identity from novice to experienced worker;
- a constellation of social, physical and textual practices, which enables knowing about work practice and facilitates the development of a workplace identity;
- a connector to learning about workplace practice and profession by facilitating the engagement between information sites that relate to conceptual knowledge and information sites that relate to embodied knowing.

In addition I view information literacy as:

- situational and driven by the need to access information contained within the symbols and artefacts and obtained through interactions; these are central and significant to the shared understanding, meaning and expression of identity, practice and profession; and
- a problematic and often highly contested practice, because information landscapes are socially, politically and historically constituted and this influence shapes information and the type of knowledge and information behaviours and activities that are valued.

Two themes emerge from Lloyd's work

Two major themes emerged from the emergency service studies. These themes reveal the similarities of experience and use of information in the workplaces of frontline emergency services practitioners and the power of information literacy to act as a transformative practice. In the first theme, *learning to act as practitioner*, outcomes of an experience with codified sources of information (e.g. text) are illustrated. The second theme *learning to become a practitioner* illustrates how the changing experience with information occurs when the novice moves away from the context-independent safety of the training context and towards contextual engagement with the workplace community and the information modalities and information activities it sanctions.

Learning to act as a practitioner

In their preparatory training both fire fighting and ambulance novices must undertake formalized competency-based training, which is assessable against the specific standards of each of the employing service organizations. In this early stage of workplace learning, the information environment of novices is deliberative and protective (Flyvbjerg, 2001) and is removed from the realities and uncertainties of actual workplace practice. The context independent nature of this preparatory environment centres on codified sources of information with a focus on individual attainment of skills and competency. Information in this environment is abstract, generalizable and can be reproduced and restated and is, therefore, assessable. Novices learn to recognize factual information and adopt information behaviours that are relevant for the acquisition of skills and competencies they are required to pass. However, because preparatory training occurs away from the workplace, in training centres or vocational colleges, this recognition and experience of information occurs without reference to concrete situations. Novices engage with this organizationally provided information in order to learn the rules, regulations, procedures and sanctioned practices of their service organization. Performance is evaluated against the existing statements described by rules, regulations, training manuals, policy and technical documents and competency-based assessments. The outcome of this engagement is the development of a subjective workplace identity, which can be recognized by the organization and by other practitioners and places novices on the periphery of the community of practice (Wenger, 1998).

Connecting with this type of information assists the newcomer with the construction of individual subjectivity, a sense of self and an understanding of their relationship to the formal organization and its agreed practices of work (Weedon, 1997). By engaging with information from these sources, newcomers are also positioned in relation to the power structures within the institutional discourse. In effect, engaging with codified sources of information allows the novice to become an effect or product of the discourse and is recognized by the workplace community (Morris and Beckett, 2004).

By engaging with institutional modalities of information, novices learn to *act as practitioners*, and develop the 'know-why' of knowledge (Billett, 2001, p. 85) but they cannot *become practitioners* because they are removed from the reflexive and reflective embodied experiences and tensions arising from practice. They are also removed from connecting with the community of workplace practitioners whose nuanced understanding of work performance is embedded within the social narratives of practice. In preparatory training, corporeal information prepares the novice's body for routine work through the rehearsal of procedural practice, but cannot prepare the novice body for the actual performance of real work because it is removed from the uncertainties of actual practice.

Similarly, while in training there is limited engagement with social modalities of information that will produce the level of intersubjectivity crucial for learning team performance and engaging with the shared sense of meaning, which is fundamental to the development of a professionally recognized identity. In the preparatory stages, social connections are made with trainers and educators whose primary role is to afford opportunities for novices to engage with the workplace-training environment. Trainers mediate and influence the novice's information engagement towards the epistemic understandings of practice that will produce successful assessable outcomes. However, once novices are assigned to workplaces, these understandings are often contested, because they may not reflect the nuanced or embodied workplace understanding, which is gained through actual work and engagement with members of the community.

This preparatory stage is important for novices because the modalities of information that are engaged with in the training centre, although abstract, allows them to develop a workplace identity that is recognizable, in organizational terms, and brings them to the periphery of actual practice. However, it is not until they engage with the community that they begin the process of developing a full workplace identity and can become an information literate worker.

Becoming a practitioner

On being assigned to their stations, novices commence the process of engaging with information from an altered discourse, one that reflects the collective perceptions of practice, profession and competency, cultural values and group history. This discourse is collective and has been constructed and agreed upon through access to everyday experiential and social information. Experienced practitioners expressed the importance of social and physical information experiences as critical in providing information that is central to the development of their performance and understandings of professional practice. One study has argued (Lloyd and Somerville, 2006) that as an intersubjective experience, workplace learning must include recognition of the body as a central information source, which facilities reflection and reflexivity. In addition the socio-cultural practices of the workplace are also recognized by practitioners as critical information sources that connect workers through shared experiences and render shared understandings about place and practice.

The acquisition of this type of information is largely informal, acquired through participation or communication between members and constituted through the development of social relations that underpin teamwork. For novices and experienced officers the value of social information lies in its application and use. By engaging with the conversations of collective practice, novices are able to move towards developing an intersubjective understanding of information that facilitates a collective view of work and of workplace practice. Learning about this source of information and how to access, interrogate and evaluate it is largely 'invisible work' and enables learning to occur 'on the job rather than off the job' (Eraut, 2004, p. 249).

Becoming a practitioner is not only achieved through the acquisition of codified or social information. It also requires the coupling of these forms of information with physical information. Coupling is central to the transition from novice to experienced practitioner. It is the process whereby information accessed from textual sites, from social sites and from the physical experience of authentic practice is drawn together, rendering the recruit in place. Therefore, physical information is central to becoming information literate in this workplace.

Physical information is central to the developing relationships between novices and experts. As a source of information, bodies provide their novice owners with a collection point for sensory information gained through actual experience. Importantly, bodies provide a narrative of this experience or lack of experience for others to see; therefore, they become an important source of information for others as well. Experienced workers observe novice bodies for *information gaps* and then use their own bodies to fill those gaps in, by demonstrating the missing information.

Practitioners, through their experience, recognize that the textual site is important for developing a preparatory framework for practice. However, once engaged with actual practice, these sites are deemed less important and can become contestable against the information experiences of embodied performance and the development of real workplace relationships. The relationship between people in the information literacy process is illustrated in Figure 4.1.

In the preparatory stage of training, the information environment is driven by codified sources of information in which the rules, regulations, policies and procedures for practice are outlined for the novice by the institution. Engaging with epistemic knowledge allows the novice to be positioned by the institution through the formation of institutional identity. Information practice is mediated by experienced trainers who guide the novice to appropriate sources of information that enable them to pass the competency-based training requirements. As part of the mediating role, information is also interpreted by experienced trainers on

Figure 4.1   Illustrates workplace information literacy for the groups studied. Adapted from Lloyd-Zantiotis (2004)

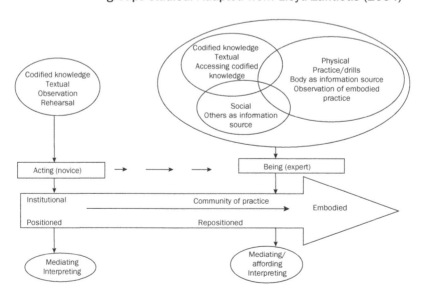

behalf of novices who, because of their lack of experience, are yet to contextualize their practice. In the transition to the workplace, novices engage with an environment that has been altered through the embodied knowledge that can only be gained through the experience of practice and long association with the culture. Apart from the codified sources, the information modalities are broadened to include social (tacit information that is nuanced towards the collective interpretation of practice and profession) and physical information, which is gained as part of the performance of duties (and includes the routine as well as the unexpected). Experienced officers act in a mediating and interpreting role, providing affordances for novices to engage with the culture of practice, and with the embodied knowledge that comes from long exposure to workplace situations. It is through this interaction, that novices' professional identity is reshaped to better reflect the nuanced understanding of the collective. This engagement, while reinforcing institutional understanding, acts to reposition novices towards the socially shared mutual understandings of the group and the culturally shared understandings of the emergency service culture. The development of effective information skills is also directed by the collective, who sanction particular forms of information access while disputing the veracity of other forms.

Such practices (although the term information literacy practice is not used) are also evident in the first piece of research into the information practice of a blue-collar worker, a vault worker in a Canadian power company (Veinot, 2007). Social practice theory was used to 'understand the social organization of workplace actions' (p. 159). Similar to my own work, Veinot used the concepts of embodiment and the situated context to understand the information practice of this worker. Different from my work, Veinot's worker creates 'boundary objects' that provide information for other administrative and maintenance workers that guide them to take actions. These 'boundary objects' connect and co-ordinate 'a range of organizational activities, thus satisfying a range of organizational information requirements' (p. 162). In discussing this, Veinot states that 'Kelly's (the vault inspector) reports act as a tool that co-ordinates the works of others, data for statistical analysis, a basis for planning new vaults, and a resource for resolving problems of equipment failure' (p. 172).

As such, Veinot (2007, p. 172) sees 'vault inspection work as an information practice'. The range of activities that this practice encompasses includes: situated judgement (using judgement in relation to rules and regulations based on previous experience and knowledge);

educated perception (of the visual environment); finding and navigating to the locations; and classification (using situated judgement and knowledge to ascertain the degree of problem discovered, or lack thereof). For example:

> Kelly uses her understanding of both the equipment and her organizational context in applying the rules and works with her colleagues to find local solutions to problems with rule application. Kelly's work is an embodied practice, where she uses educated perceptual skills, navigational skills, and situated judgment to observe and classify phenomena. Moreover the chief mandate of vault inspectors is to produce a report that connects and coordinates the work of a range of other players within the power company. (p. 173)

Exploring the nature of information practice among nurses in Sweden, Johannisson and Sundin (2007) draw on the concept of neopragmatism in order to advocate information practice as a social practice. The authors acknowledged the relevance of 'communicative participation' between participants given that library and information studies research is based on communication. Nurses in this study were seen to have 'context bound dealings' (p. 200); this reflects much of the literature on workplace information literacy as being context specific. Nurses discussed their, and other nurses', information use, seeking, evaluation and in some instances production of text, irrespective of format (e.g. documents, articles, books and websites) but one within the context of being a professional 'community of justification', i.e. one that is 'permeated by power relations' (p. 204) and 'making specific knowledge claims as to what should be included or excluded from the specific area of expertise' (p. 203). The authors' analysis revealed at least two levels of discourse that promoted specific interests of the profession: '... the science-oriented medical discourse and the more holistically oriented nursing discourse were two tools employed in the nurses' accounts of their attitudes toward the production and use of professional information (Johannisson and Sundin, 2007, p. 215).

Commenting on the relationship between medical and nursing knowledge, the authors see the specific positions of nurses and doctors are fixed according to a specific knowledge hierarchy.

The research of the above authors demonstrates that research into information literacy can extend beyond the skills-based approach. However, further work is needed in this area in order to develop the rich descriptions that lead to conceptualizing information literacy practice as a complex process that extends beyond experiencing information through text.

Issues for workplace information literacy

The concept of information literacy as a set of 'generic skills', a theme often promoted in the educational sector, is brought into question in workplace research and leads us to ask, does information literacy taught in one context transfer to another context? The substantial body of literature in cognitive and situated learning studies, which has examined transfer of learning, appears inconclusive on the issue. This is primarily related to whether a cognitive or situated learning perspective is adopted. From a cognitive perspective, there are some strong arguments that suggest that in some aspects of transfer the answer is 'no'. Alternatively, from a socio-cultural perspective, which emphasize co-participation and context, the answer is not so clear-cut because of the recognition of the importance of other people within the workplace and the affording opportunities for learning to occur. Both positions have implications for arguments about the transfer of information literacy as a suite of generic skills lifted from the education context into the workplace.

Transfer is defined by Detterman (1993, p. 4) as 'the degree to which behaviour will be repeated in a new situation'. While this appears a simple definition, Detterman conceptualizes transfer as a continuum. Along this continuum is *near transfer*, which describes the transfer of skills that can occur if the context or situation is similar, e.g. learning to drive a truck after learning to drive a car (Misko, 1998). However, Misko (1998) argues that this distinction may not be as straightforward as this. In a study of the ability of a group of students to retain knowledge and skills in one context and to reproduce the knowledge and skills in a new context, Misko (1998) reported that 'there was no guarantee that being able to perform a skill in one context means being able to transfer the skill to another' (p. 298).

The importance of situated activity has been strengthened by Greeno *et al.* (1993). They draw on socio-cultural and ecological theories in their analysis of learning transfer to suggest that the conditions for transfer are dependent on 'a person's having learned to participate in an activity in a socially constructed domain of situations that includes the situation where transfer can occur' (p. 161). This view of transfer focuses on the situational factors, the structure of an activity and the social interactions that occur during initial learning and transfer (p. 161). Gerber and Oaklief (2000) argue that the tendency to take an academic approach to transfer (i.e. to seek commonality in skill or competency) tends to produce an 'overgeneralised, decontextualised approach to workplace learning that does not prize the relationships that develop among work teams …' (p. 179).

In considering information literacy transfer, it appears that *near transfer* may only be possible and demonstrable when the information literacy practices as they are currently taught in an educational context, transfer into similar educational contexts, i.e. through the different years of university education or from university or discipline-oriented workplaces. Information literacy skills taught in an educational context and relating to educational practices may not be easily transferable to training contexts (i.e. TAFE) or workplace contexts that have their own idiosyncrasies in terms of practices and information dissemination, ones that inform learning about work performance. In this respect, developing an understanding grounded in novice and expert learning may better inform our own practices and help facilitate the possibility of information literacy transfer out of the educational context and into workplace learning performance. It will also provide an understanding of what is actually being transferred and at what level of competency this is occurring.

In the fire fighter study (Lloyd-Zantiotis, 2004) transfer from *acting as a fire fighter* (subjective position) to *being a fire fighter* (intersubjective position) is achieved through the development of information-related practices. These are afforded by experts who observe novice practice, identify gaps in their learning, and provide opportunities for novices to access information about the practices of work through guidance, scaffolding and coaching (Billett, 2001). They also require the novice to actively reflect on the affordances in the context of their learning. These activities facilitate the repositioning of the novice away from institutionally sanctioned sites of knowledge, towards the sites of knowledge and the information practices that are valued by the fire fighter's platoon. These practices act as opportunities to mediate and afford information, thus enabling *near transfer* and transition from an institutional context to a collective practice and the development of collective competencies.

The issue of transfer appears critical for information literacy practitioners, if they are to continue to define information literacy as a critical practice and as a prerequisite for lifelong learning (Bundy, 2004) outside of tertiary contexts. Within the context of the workplace information use of university administrative workers, Hepworth and Smith (2008, p. 227) concur with Bundy's view when they state that:

> ... there is a gap between librarians' and LIS academics' conceptions of the skills associated with information literacy that stem from the school and higher education context and the experience of information literacy in the workplace. This is partly because the terminology we use is unfamiliar to people in the workplace but also because of the hierarchical and collaborative nature of work which means that information literacies may be distributed among the work group.

In a study of information literacy training for Australian students studying engineering, Palmer and Tucker (2004), argued that, while information literacy may be referred to as a generic skill because it is seen to underpin all forms of learning, it is not essentially a 'global, context-free attribute' (p. 19). This is primarily because experiencing an information landscape and learning how to use the information resources available will depend on developing an understanding of the unique and idiosyncratic characteristics of the context. McMahon and Bruce (2002), following their investigation of development workers' perceptions of local staff information literacy needs, concluded that danger lies in 'imposing ... another "outside" view of what local workers need' (p. 22), suggesting that current educationally driven conceptions of information literacy and information literacy practices may not reflect the nature or manifestation in other contexts. They also suggested that: 'The enabling of local workers to navigate the dominant systems and its associated workplace structures, to access information relevant for their local community, to translate it into their local community context and to communicate it effectively in culturally appropriate ways, are all elements of a project which addresses the information literacy needs of those workers' (McMahon and Bruce, 2002, p. 125).

Bevan (2003) argues that while information literacy skills may be validated from a conceptual level as generic skills, this labelling of information literacy falls down at the concrete or operational level. This is because it fails to take into account the nuances and social practices involved in the application and practice of information literacy in a context-dependent setting. Exploring information literacy from three research sites and in the context of three specific practices—airline customer service, efficient use of software and use of hypermedia—Bevan concludes that 'In summary, it informs us that conceiving of information literacy as a "generic skill" that can be separately identified and taught has a tendency to both trivialize its complexity and devalue its importance in the development of workplace skills' (p. 130).

Kirk's (2004) investigation of managers' ways of experiencing information led her to suggest that: 'the complexity of information use raises questions about the education and training of people for the workplace. IL programmes in schools, TAFE colleges and universities have usually assumed a limited experience of information use and a limited understanding of information' (p. 197).

The need to dispel assumptions about the perception that people come to a workplace with an already developed cache of information skills and competencies has already been highlighted by Crawford and Irving (2007). Crawford and Irving had been exploring the link between information literacy in secondary and tertiary education and the implications for the workplace. These authors highlighted in their research that while employers generally believe that employees will come to them with information-related skills and competencies, the ad hoc nature of information skill and competency development in further or higher education or at work often results in poorly developed skills and the perception that these skills will adequately equip the employee for work. Crawford and Irving (2007, p. 23) suggest that: 'It is important therefore to dispel the assumptions that everyone has these skills and competencies at a level that they need, that they are explicitly and uniformly taught within education or are learned in conjunction with information and communication technology or by osmosis'.

Studies on information literacy transfer are still emerging. However, recent research (Ellis and Salisbury, 2004, p. 191) on library skills transfer indicates that library skills training, which may occur in schools, 'does not appear to be transferred readily into the university environment'. Similarly, Hartmann (2001) reported that the school library experience was unhelpful to students moving into university environments because of different curriculum expectations.

In considering the concept of transfer in relation to information skills, Markless and Streatfield (2006) argue that more attention needs to be focused on the conditions for transfer (i.e. information literacy skills) should be practised in a variety of contexts and that studies should be encouraged to engage students in reflexive practice (i.e. thinking about their information practices and monitoring their own learning in relation to this). The increase in online learning at tertiary and vocational levels will also prove problematic to many workplaces that expect new workers to arrive work ready with a range of skills including the ability to work collectively. Markless and Streatfield (2006) also point out that the disconnected and isolated nature of this learning tends not to foster the deep reflection and critical analysis needed to encourage transfer (p. 23).

Use of information literacy standards and guidelines

While no specific information literacy standards have been developed for the workplace, some attempts have been made to adapt the education standards and guidelines to the workplace. Kirton *et al.* (2008) found that special librarians showed that they 'recognise the published (ANZIIL) standards of information literacy' (p. 252). In particular, Standards One (recognize need), Two (find information), Three (critically evaluate) and Six (understand the social and legal use of information) were included in the authors' analysis of information literacy. However, with Standard Four (manages information) and Standard Five (constructs new knowledge from new and prior) there was a more varied response, possibly reflecting the nature of the workplace.

Comparing the ACRL standards with information literacy needs in the workplace, Cheuk (2002) argues that business leaders and policy makers might find the standards useful to promote the practice in the workplace. In presenting this argument Cheuk compared the standards and lists of information literacy skills lacking in the workplace. However, this comparison is only aimed at tertiary-trained employees and reflects the higher education discourse that centres information literacy practice around the research process and the individuals' ability to develop skills that will enable access to objective knowledge through print or digital-based technologies. While this may be suitable for knowledge workers, it does not account for information literacy practice as it is realized by workers without tertiary education. For example, the notion that being information literate requires the ability to identify an information need, is without foundation in the workplace as the majority of workers will have their information needs determined by more experienced practitioners or supervisors. Similarly the notion of plagiarism, while an important scholarly issue and relevant for knowledge workers, is largely unrecognized in other workplace sectors that rely on collaborative thinking and the sharing of ideas often without concern for provenance. The reified and abstract portrayal of information literacy in educational settings is incongruent with the actual account of the practice of information literacy in the workplace and this issue requires urgent attention from researchers, especially if educational settings are serious about preparing people for the workplace.

Characteristics of information literacy in the workplace

The workplace landscape is complex and messy and research relating to information literacy while still emerging in this sector has begun to illustrate features of information literacy not identified in the educational setting. As in the education sector, the prevailing and current focus of information literacy research is still centralized around information skills, which also indicates the influence of the educational discourse across sectors. However, it also suggests that more research is required in order for information literacy to be fully understood. None the less, the education sector also benefits from a more sociological approach to their understanding of information literacy, which has drawn on research into workplace learning in order to frame the practice for this sector.

In reviewing the literature related to workplace information literacy a number of themes could be seen to characterize this landscape, each relating to ways in which information and knowledge are perceived. When information and knowledge are understood to be *external* and *objective*, information literacy practice manifests in this sector as:

- a list of skills or competencies that are reproducible, restatable and therefore measurable;
- reflecting the same information skills learned in the educational context;
- focused around codified sources of written information (e.g. training manual, rules, regulations, competency based assessment practices); and
- focused on the reproduction of a subjective institutional identity.

However, when information and knowledge are seen as a *construction* and are *relational* to the ongoing collaborative practices of people who work in consort with one another a number of other features are revealed. These challenge the prevailing concept of information literacy as skills-based literacy and illustrate the complexity and depth of the practice. This understanding of information literacy practice is not focused on *how* information literacy is operationalized but why. When information literacy is understood from this perspective a number of other features are revealed, which are a recognition that:

- information literacy practice is not centred around a single information modality, but also has social and physical dimensions;

- information literacy is a collective rathe...
  - the intersubjective nature of informat...
    whereby an emphasis is placed on unde...
    information and knowledge in the contex...
    its practices and ensuring that informati...
    development of shared meaning;
  - emphasis is, therefore, placed on the commu...
    role ensuring that new members engage with...
    valued according to the norms, beliefs a...
    community;
- the experience of information is influenced by the ...
  political and economic arrangements that have influen...
  the setting;
- information need not be highlighted through individua...
  e.g. workers often have their information need defined ...
  experienced workers—this is in contrast with the education...
  of information literacy, where the information need is ...
  understanding information literacy practice in this setting;
- workers are less reliant on secondary sources—more empi...
  placed on the experiential and embodied information that come...
  direct practice and is employed in the development of mutually sl...
  understandings about practice;
- an understanding of critical evaluation does not mirror textu...
  understandings but is more reflective of workplace practice;
- there is a stronger focus on collaboration, teamwork and development...
  of shared understanding about practice and performance;
- there is an emphasis on reflexivity (reflection on action in practice)
  and greater understanding of praxis;
- that developing expertise is an ongoing and continual process; and
- codified sources of knowledge are not the only sanctioned source—
  information drawn from social and physical modalities is important
  in workplace learning.

Conclusions

In the workplace the skills view of information literacy still prevails and
is influenced by the education sector's transmission and training of

based paradigm. However, the socio-cultural view of information
y, which is emerging from empirical research in the workplace
r indicates that information literacy is more complex than the sum
skills. In the workplace sector learning has both formal and informal
ities and involves accessing information that is not only explicit and
bound, but also information that is tacit and nuanced in the socio-
tural, historical and material features of the site. Therefore, we need to
velop an understanding of what constitutes information, how and why
is shared, and which modalities are sanctioned by those who engage
ith the performance and practice of work and workplace learning.

References

Association of College and Research Libraries (ACRL). (2000). Information literacy competency standards for higher education [Electronic Version]. Retrieved from http://www.ala.org/ala/acrl/acrlstandards/informationliteracycompetency.html/.

Bennet, A. (2004). Information literacy: a new basic competency. *CHIPS Magazine*, Fall 2(X) I. Retrieved January 2009 from http://www.chips.navy.mil/archives/01_fall/information_literacy.htm

Bevan, F. (2003). Developing information literacy In J. Stevenson (Ed.), *Developing vocational expertise* (pp. 110–134). Crows Nest, Australia: Allen and Unwin.

Billett, S. (2001). *Learning in the workplace; strategies for effective practice*. Crows Nest, NSW: Allen and Unwin.

Boon, S., Johnston, B. and Webber, S. (2007). A phenomenographic study of English faculty's conceptions of information literacy. *Journal of Documentation*, 63(2), 204–228.

Breivik, P. (1985). Putting libraries back in the information society. *American Libraries*, 16(10), 723.

Breivik, P. (2005). 21st century learning and information literacy. *Change*, 37(2), 21–27.

Bruce, C. (1996). *Information literacy; a phenomenongraphy*. Unpublished PhD, University of New England. Armidale, NSW.

Bruce, C. (1997). *The seven faces of information literacy*. Blackwood, S.A: Auslib Press.

Bruce, C. (1999). Workplace experiences of information literacy. *International Journal of Information Management*, 19, 33–47.

Bundy, A. (2004). *Australian and New Zealand Information Literacy Framework: principles, standards and practice* (2nd ed.). Australian and New Zealand Institute for Information Literacy.

Burnheim, R. (1992). Information literacy: a core competency. *Australian Academic and Research Libraries*, 23(4), 188–196.

Cheuk, B. (1998). Exploring information literacy in the workplace: a qualitative study of engineers using sense-making approach. *International Forum on Information and Documentation*, 23(2), 30–38.

Cheuk, W. B. (2000). Exploring information literacy in the workplace: a process approach. In C. Bruce and P. Candy (Eds), *Information literacy around the world: advances in programs and research* (pp. 177–192). Wagga Wagga, NSW: Centre for Information Studies.

Cheuk, W. B. (2002). *Information literacy in the workplace context: issues, best practices and challenges.* White Paper prepared for UNESCO, the US National Forum on Information Literacy Meeting of Experts, Prague, The Czech Republic, July. Retrieved 22 June 2004 from http://74.11.214.110/libinter/infolitconf&meet/papers/cheuk-fullpaper.pdf.

Cohen, D. (1998). *Managing knowledge in the new economy.* New York: The Conference Board.

Crawford, J. and Irving, C. (2007). Information literacy: the link between secondary and tertiary education project and its wider implications. *Journal of Librarianship and Information Science*, 39(1), 17–26.

Crawford, J. and Irving, C. (2009). Information literacy in the workplace: a qualitative exploratory study. *Journal of Librarianship and Information Science*, 41(1), 29–38.

De Saulles, M. (2007). Information literacy among UK SMEs: an information policy gap. *Aslib Proceedings: New Information Perspectives*, 59(1), 68–97.

Dervin, B. (1992). From the mind's eye of the 'user': the sense-making qualitative-quantitative methodology. In J. D. Glazier and R. R. Powell (Eds), *Qualitative research in information management* (pp. 61–84). Englewood, CO: Libraries Unlimited.

Detterman, D. (1993). The case for the prosecution: transfer as an epiphenomenon. In D. K. Detterman and R. J. Sternberg (Eds), *Transfer on trial; intelligence, cognition and instruction* (pp. 1–24). Norwood, NJ: Ablex Publishing.

Economist Intelligence Unit. (2007). *In search of clarity: unravelling the complexities of executive decision making.* A report from the Economist Intelligence Unit. 1–21. Retrieved 20 December 2008 from http://www.businessobjects.com/jump/emea/economist/report/EIU_In_search_of_clarity_8_August_2007.pdf/.

Ellis, J. and Salisbury, F. (2004). Information literacy milestones: building upon the prior knowledge of first-year students. *The Australian Library Journal*, 53(4), 383–394.

Eraut, M. (2004). Informal learning in the workplace. *Studies in Continuing Education*, 26(2), 248–273.

Fafeita, J. (2005). *Taking the pulse ... the information literacy practices of Victorian TAFE librarians*. Paper presented at the Research Applications in Information and Library Studies Seminar (RAILS 2): Proceedings of the 2nd Research Applications in Information and Library Studies Seminar, held at the National Library of Australia, Canberra, 16–17 September 2005.

Finn, B. (Chair) (1991). *Young people's participation in post compulsory education and training*. Australian Education Council Review Committee. Canberra: Australian Government Publishing Service.

Flyvbjerg, B. (2001). *Making social science matter: why social inquiry fails and how it can succeed again*. Cambridge: Cambridge University Press.

Gasteen, G. and O'Sullivan, C. (2000). Working towards the information literate law firm. In C. Bruce and P. Candy (Eds), *Information literacy around the world: advances in programs and research* (pp. 109–120). Wagga Wagga, Australia: Centre for Information Studies, Charles Sturt University.

Gerber, R. and Oaklief, C. (2000). Transfer of learning to strengthen workplace training. In R. Gerber and C. Lankshear (Eds), *Training for a smart workforce* (pp. 176–192). London: Routledge.

Greeno, J., Moore, J. and Smith, D. (1993). Transfer of situated learning. In D. K. Detterman and J. R. Sternberg (Eds). *Transfer on trial: intelligence, cognition and instruction* (pp. 99–167). Norwood, NJ: Ablex Publishing.

Hartmann, E. (2001). Understandings of information literacy: the perceptions of first year undergraduate students at the University of Ballarat. *Australian Academic and Research Libraries*, 32(2), 110–122.

Hepworth, M. and Smith, M. (2008). Workplace Information literacy for administrative staff in higher education. *Australian Library Journal*, 57(3), 212–236.

Irving, C. and Crawford, J. (2008). *A national information literacy framework Scotland*. Retrieved September 12, 2008, from http://www.caledonian.ac.uk/ils/framework.html/.

Johannisson, J. and Sundin, O. (2007). Putting discourse to work: information practices and the professional project of nurses. *Library Quarterly*, 2(77), 199–218.

Kapitzke, S. (2003). Information literacy: a positivist epistemology and politics of outformation. *Educational Theory*, 53(1), 37–53.

Kirk, J. (2004). Tumble dryers and juggernaughts: information-use processes in organizations. In P. Danaher, C. Macpherson, F. Nouwens and D. Orr (Eds), *Lifelong learning: Whose responsibility and what is your contribution?* Proceedings of the 3rd International Lifelong Learning Conference, Yeppoon, Queensland, Australia, 13–16 June (pp. 192–197) Rockhampton: Central Queensland University Press.

Kirton, J., Barham, L. and Brady, S. (2008). Understanding and practice of information literacy in Australian government libraries. *Australian Library Journal*, 57(3), 237–256.

Lloyd, A. (2003). Information literacy: the metacompetency of the knowledge economy: an exploratory paper. *Journal of Librarianship and Information Science*, 35(2), 87–92.

Lloyd, A. (2005a). Information literacy; different contexts, different concepts, different truths? *Journal of Librarianship and Information Science*, 37(2), 82–88.

Lloyd, A. (2005b). No man (or woman) is an island: information literacy, affordances and communities of practice. *Australian Library Journal*, 54(3), 230–237.

Lloyd, A. (2006a). *Drawing from others; ways of knowing about information literacy performance.* Paper presented at the lifelong learning: partners, pathways and pedagogies. Keynote and refereed papers from the 4th International Lifelong Learning Conference, Rockhampton: Central Queensland.

Lloyd, A. (2006b). Information literacy landscapes: an emerging picture. *Journal of Documentation*, 62(5), 570–583.

Lloyd, A. (2007). Recasting information literacy as sociocultural practice: implications for library and information science researchers" *Information Research*, 12(4). Retrieved June 2008 from http://InformationR.net/ir/12-4/colis34.html/.

Lloyd, A. and Somerville, M (2005). Working information. *Journal of Workplace Learning*, 18(3), 186–198.

Lloyd, A. and Williamson, K. (2008). Towards and understanding of information literacy in context: implications for research. *Journal of Librarianship and Information Science*, 40(1), 3–12.

Lloyd-Zantiotis, A. (2004). *Working information: a grounded theory of information literacy in the workplace.* Unpublished, University of New England, Armidale, NSW.

Markless, S. and Streatfield, D. (2006). Three decades of information literacy: redefining the parameters. In S. Andretta (Ed.), *Change and challenge: information literacy for the 21st century* (pp. 15–36). Blackwood, SA: Auslib Press.

Mayer, E. (1992). *Putting general education to work: the key competencies report.* Canberra: Australian Education Council and Ministers for Vocational Education and Training.

McMahon, C. and Bruce, C. (2002). Information literacy needs of local staff in cross-cultural development projects. *International Journal of Community Development*, 14, 113–127.

Misko, J. (1998). Do skills transfer? An empirical study. Paper presented at the *VET research influencing policy and practice*. Proceedings of the first national conference of the Australian Vocational Education and Training Research Association, Sydney.

Morris, G. and Beckett, D. (2004). Learning for/at work: Somali women 'Doing it for themselves'. *Journal of Workplace Learning*, 16(1/2), 75–82.

Mutch, A. (2000). Information literacy: a critical realists perspective. In C. Bruce and P. Candy (Eds), *Information literacy around the world: advances in programs and research* (pp. 152–162). Wagga Wagga: Centre for Information Studies.

Oman, J. (2001). Information literacy in the workplace. *Information Outlook*, 5, 6. Retrieved 23 December 2008 from http://www.sla.org/content/Shop/Information/infoonline/2001/jun01/oman.cfm/.

O'Sullivan, C. (2002). Is information literacy relevant for the real world. *Reference Services Review*, 30(1), 7–14.

Palmer, S. and Tucker, B. (2004). Planning, delivery and evaluation of information literacy training for engineering and technology students. *Australian Academic and Research Libraries*, March, 13–33.

Rosenberg, V. (2002). *Information literacy and small business.* White Paper prepared for UNESCO, the US National Commission on Libraries and Information Science, and the National Forum on Information Literacy, for use at the Information Literacy Meeting of Experts, Prague, The Czech Republic. Retrieved 30 November 2008 from http://74.11.214.110/libinter/infolitconf&meet/papers/rosenberg-fullpaper.pdf/.

Smith, E. and Martina, C. (2004). Keeping the dough rising: considering information in the workplace with reference to the bakery trade. In P. Danaher, C. Macpherson, F. Nouwens and D. Orr (Eds), *Lifelong learning: Whose responsibility and what is your contribution?* Proceedings of the 3rd International Lifelong Learning Conference, Yeppoon, Queensland, Australia, 13–16 June (pp. 325–329). Rockhampton: Central Queensland University Press.

Stevenson, J. (2002). Concepts of workplace knowledge. *Educational Research,* 37, 1–15.

Tovey, M. D. (1997). *Training in Australia: design, delivery, evaluation, management.* Frenches Forest, Australia: Prentice Hall.

Veinot, T. (2007) The eyes of the power company; workplace information practices of a vault inspector. *Library Quarterly,* 77(2), 157–179.

Webb, J. and Powis, C. (2004). *Teaching information skills: theory and practice.* London: Facet Publishing.

Weedon, C. (1997). *Feminism, theory and the politics of difference.* Oxford: Blackwell.

Wenger, E. (1998). *Communities of practice; learning, meaning and identity.* Cambridge; Cambridge University Press.

Zurkowski, P. (1974). *The information service environment: relationships and priorities.* ED 100391. National Commission on Libraries and Information Science, Washington DC: ERIC Clearinghouse on Information Resources.

5

Information literacy advocacy and the public library landscape

Introduction

The importance of information literacy, in relation to lifelong learning; enabling a more informed and empowered citizenry; and, addressing the inequalities produced by the information society, has been strongly advocated at an international level. Endorsement by UNESCO (United Nations Educational, Scientific and Cultural Organization) through the Prague Declaration (2003) and the Alexandria Proclamation (Garner 2006) has seen the concept of information literacy become widely disseminated among the library community. As a result, a discourse has been created that establishes the values of information literacy and situates the practice as a critical literacy in the twenty-first century (Garner, 2006).

However, despite the importance of the declarations and the widespread dissemination to the broader community, there has been minimal research conducted in public library and community landscapes. A number of reasons may contribute to this lacuna. First, while it is possible to clearly articulate what information literacy should do for an individual and how it contributes to their practice, it is often difficult to articulate what information literacy is without resorting to abstraction and generalization or simply falling back to the skills and information and communication technology literacy paradigm. This is because information literacy, as we have seen in the other landscapes, will manifest itself differently according to the situation in which it is practised. While we continue to focus on the individual, it is the setting and the collaborative practices that shape the setting that should be the object of our attention. As community settings are so broad, there appears to be a difficulty in reconciling the aspirational statements of information literacy, which are generalized and abstract, with the realities of actual practice. Secondly, while these statements do not explicitly connect information literacy with the digital age, there are implicit assumptions that technology is the primary mode and model for communication and to be without it is to be part of the information literate poor. This view produces a deficit model of information literacy—one where the focus is on the *tools* of learning and communication, rather than the *holistic* nature of information and learning. Finally, evidence from the literature in this sector appears to suggest that public and community librarians feel that the 'championing' of information literacy has been imposed upon them, with little professional or financial support. While it is clear that they accept this responsibility, the complex and unbounded nature of information literacy in this sector makes it difficult for this particular group to conceptualize the unique characteristics of information literacy for the many groups within this sector. This leads to difficulty in developing cohesive and effective information literacy programmes. Consequently, information literacy education for this sector tends to draw on some elements from the educational sector, and is usually reduced to technology training and information searching.

Where research has been conducted it appears to be aimed at understanding and highlighting the need and implications of information literacy practice for lifelong learning or the lack of librarians' skills or training. However, the most interesting feature of this landscape is the reflexive understanding whereby public librarians are examining their own skills and expertise (or lack of these) in relation to their ability to develop information literacy skills in others.

Advocacy of information literacy

Advocacy for information literacy has been located in the majority of international peak bodies that represent the library, cultural and education sectors. Prominent among these are the United Nations Educational, Scientific, and Cultural Organization (UNESCO) Information for All Programme (IFAP). Two significant documents have been produced by UNESCO, these are the Prague Declaration (NCLIS, 2003) and the Alexandria Proclamation (Garner, 2006). These documents make explicit the discourse of information literacy as an enabling information practice, which contributes to the empowerment of citizens, and they illustrate a range of views about what should constitute information literacy practice. The work of the international committees has contributed to the development of curriculum documents employed in the education sector, e.g. US Association of College and Research Libraries (ACRL), the UK Society of College, National and University Libraries (SCONUL) and the Australian and New Zealand Institute for Information Literacy (ANZIIL). Peak bodies representing the sector have also adopted the principles and objectives, e.g. American Library Association (ALA), and the Australian Library and Information Association (ALIA). There is some doubt as to the effectiveness of these groups in raising the profile of information literacy outside of the education sector, in particular, in the workplace or within the areas of government policy, which appears to still consider information literacy to only be an information and communication technology-related skill.

The key value underpinning the development of the Alexandria Proclamation is the force of information literacy and lifelong learning as powerful agents to promote social inclusion, empowerment and democratization for the world's people in today's information society. Embedded in the Alexandria Proclamation is the intention to raise the 'global awareness of information literacy as part of the human right to lifelong learning' (Garner, 2006, p. 5). Patricia Breivik, the Chair Emeritus of The National Forum on Information Literacy, summarized the relationship and importance of these two key events in Prague and Alexandria by indicating that: 'The outcomes of the Prague event laid the theoretical foundation for international collaboration in promoting Information Literacy as an essential set of abilities in the 21st century ... The Alexandria colloquium took those outputs and began the process of developing practical agendas for raising awareness and promoting Information Literacy and lifelong learning skills.' (Garner, 2006, p. 5).

Prior to the Alexandria colloquium an expert panel of sector experts and regional team leaders met to establish a set of 'givens'. These are useful to consider as key conceptual drivers that underpinned the meeting's set of information literacy values and established a contemporary information literacy discourse. They are stated as the following (Garner, 2006, p. 30).

- Information literacy is too important to be left to any one institution, agency or profession; collaboration is essential.
- Information literacy needs to be approached within the context of people's cultural values, societal groupings and personal information needs.

- Information literacy is more than use of technology.

- Information literacy is concerned with empowering people regardless of modes of information access and delivery.

- Achievement of information literacy goals requires flexible strategies to meet the needs of diverse communities and individuals.

- Information literacy is a prerequisite for participating effectively in the information society and is part of the basic human right of lifelong learning education.

For the Alexandria Proclamation on information literacy to be advanced at a global level Philip Candy argued that it needs to gain the status of an issue of vital world importance. This would require advocates to become more outward looking and to critically reflect on the successful features of worldwide movements. He suggests that: 'We should learn from mass education movements, whether about environment, health, smoking or appropriate sexual practices. We need to examine what has been highly successful worldwide and determine the essence of those successful interventions that we can use to promote Information Literacy' (Garner, 2006, p. 49).

An example of advocacy at this level is found in Australia where the Australian Library and Information Association (ALIA) has produced the *Statement on Information Literacy for all Australians*. Drawing from the Alexandria Proclamation (Garner, 2006), ALIA articulates the principle of information literacy as:

> A thriving national and global culture, economy and democracy will best be advanced by people who are empowered in all walks of life to seek, evaluate, use and create information effectively to achieve their personal, social, occupational and educational goals. It is a basic human right in a digital world and promotes social inclusion within a range of cultural contexts.
>
> ALIA (2006)

This statement exemplifies the discourse of information literacy for all peak organizations. Information literacy is articulated in these statements as a practice that is inclusive of all people; facilitates learning for life; enables the creation of new knowledge; is underpinned by the acquisition of skills; enables innovation and enterprise; and produces participatory citizenry, social and economic development as an outcome (NCLIS *et al.*, 2003; ALIA, 2006; Garner, 2006).

In these peak bodies' reports, information literacy is commonly defined as the ability to locate, evaluate, manage and use information. There is a strong connection between information literacy and technology, in particular the use of information and communication technology to access information and information literacy is conceptualized from a library-centric perspective. This particular view is largely organized around print-based or digitized materials and a decentralized view of information literacy as a transferable generic skill.

However, attempts to have information literacy placed on the political agendas of government bodies has proved difficult and at the time of the Alexandria Proclamation (Garner, 2006), Finland was the only country to have achieved this objective. Tovote (in Garner, 2006, p. 45) highlighted work that had been undertaken in that country, indicating that information literacy issues had reached the political level, resulting in the inclusion of information literacy programmes for all ages. In general, Nordic countries have been proactive in collaborating on information literacy projects that focus around the public library sector. An example provided by Hansen (2004) is a Nordbok funded project involving Norway, Finland, Sweden, Iceland and Denmark that explored a number of themes related to national policies and information literacy. These included public libraries as learning centres, librarians as teachers, and library strategies in relation to advocacy at all levels. A second phase of the collaborative project has resulted in the widespread dissemination of information literacy practices.

Advocacy was viewed by Bruce and Lampson (2002) as an important factor in order for information literacy to be successfully accepted. Librarians also understood the need to advocate for information literacy at the policy level by gaining support from their library's boards and administrators. The authors (p. 102) suggested that: '… librarians who are most knowledgeable and motivated regarding information literacy need to educate and motivate their administrators and co-workers and create partnerships to promote the allocation of information literacy resources in the form of staffing, and the prioritization of time and budget.'

The advocacy role of library associations and the profession

The need for the information profession to build the impetus for change by raising public awareness of information literacy has become an established theme in the literature. In particular, professional associations and their members are identified as being key players in lobbying government to establish information literacy policy, for resources and funding to enable libraries and other bodies to undertake the work of developing the infrastructure, and for staff training in order to implement programmes for the community (see, for example, the information literacy train the trainer programmes supported by UNESCO). Bundy (2002, p. 125) argues that because librarians recognize the importance of information literacy as prerequisite for 'personal and democratic empowerment', they should actively advocate to governments and educators that the critical issue of the information age is the 'information literacy divide, not the digital divide'.

Bundy couples this discourse about the empowerment of others with the characterization of information literate people, which draws from the educational perspective of information literacy. 'People who recognise their own need for good information, and who have the skills to identify, access, evaluate, synthesise and apply the needed information are thus information literate' (p. 125).

The ALA developed their paper on information literacy *Building information literate communities* (2001) along with establishing a subcommittee with the aim of 'building public awareness of what it takes to be information literate in the 21st century' (Brey-Casiano, 2006, pp. 181–190). Furthering this aim, the association produced a package for librarians to develop their information literacy advocacy skills. The package was entitled A *library advocate's guide to building information literate communities* and is available on the ALA website along with their other information literacy tools. During her term as ALA President Brey-Casiano believed that opportunities should be developed to create worldwide partnerships within the library profession to advocate for information literacy and share resources. She suggested that:

> ... we should create a *worldwide* network of library advocates who can share ideas, resources and much more. With the many resources available to us here in the United States, provided by ALA and other organizations, we can build information literate communities in every corner of the world, which provide a better quality of life for the people who live there (p. 190).

Given the lack of public money available for information literacy initiatives within the community sector, this sentiment is admirable. However, while it still appears that many attempts are being made by the various information literacy associations (e.g. ANZIIL, SCONUL, NFIL) to provide online resources, the lack of funding for information literacy training and support for the development of programmes appears to be a major hindrance for librarians within the public sector.

Information literacy in the public library sector

In comparison with the literature on information literacy in the higher education landscape there are few research studies and little written on how information literacy is conceptualized in the public library sector, in instructional programmes, or about the practitioner experience of information literacy in the public landscape (Virkus, 2003; Hart, 2006; Harding, 2008). In a recent article, Harding (2008) identified that less than 2% of the literature on information literacy has any focus on public libraries and suggests that 'little guidance has been given ... as to how they should go about this', i.e. information literacy programme development (p. 289). This useful literature review by Harding focused on the value of public libraries in relation to community information literacy developments and the progress made by public libraries in their information literacy endeavours.

Compared with the higher education sector and to a lesser extent the workplace, in public libraries, research into information literacy appears to be in the early stages of development. This is evidenced by studies examining: staff and user attitudes to information literacy (Koning, 2001; Bruce and Lampson, 2002; Julien and Hoffman, 2008); identification of the national status of information literacy development (Julien and Breu, 2005; Hart, 2006); raising concerns about the inadequacy of staff training, resources and infrastructure (Harding, 2008); levels of planning and documentation for information literacy (Harding, 2008); and advocacy and promotion (Brey-Casiano, 2006; Harding, 2008). An earlier study by Ryynanen (2002), points to the vital role of public libraries in providing equitable access to information for people with socio-economic disadvantage (i.e. those without the capacity to own the technology) for participation in the twenty-first century information society.

The notion that public libraries are well placed within the community to foster information literacy and promote the importance of an information literate society prevails in many of the peak body statements and from key writers in this area (e.g. see Breivik and Gee, 1989; Bundy,

2002). This contrasts with the idea that information literacy practice is being imposed on the public sector, and is reported by Harding (2008), who echoes the earlier statements of Julien and Hoffman (2008). Harding (2008, p. 274) states that 'despite the myriad challenges, public libraries world wide are embracing this imposed responsibility and have implemented a wide array of information literacy programs'. However, these programmes tend to mirror the library-centric view of information literacy, of combining bibliographic skills with the promotion of a skill set that reflects searching for online information using readily available search engines and databases and the use of computers.

In her analysis of the literature, Harding (2008) argues that the public library is in a strong position to facilitate information literacy skill development in the community. She identifies the strengths within the public library system (p. 279), including:

- the traditional and recognized role of the public library as a place of learning;
- that from a community perspective librarians are considered to be information experts;
- the broad client base of public libraries is a strength when it comes to fostering the information literacy message;
- the public library often represents a child's first learning experience with formal information access, and from this perspective librarians are able to instil the importance and value of information and of the library as an information space;
- that the public library has the ability to facilitate lifelong learning through their contact with members of the community who are interested in self-directed study or informal learning;
- the one-to-one relationship between public librarians and clients provides teachable moments (one-to-one reference training encounters);
- public librarians have been effective in forming partnerships with other stakeholders (e.g. schools, government). This places them in a prime position to advocate the information literacy message; and
- as key access points for general public to information and information and communication technology resources, the public library is in a strong position to provide training.

However, while public libraries appear to have accepted this imposed responsibility for information literacy instruction, Harding (2008) notes that there is a lack of information literacy guidelines and few manuals that have been developed specifically for this sector that take into account the realities of the practice or client need. This author also points to the issues of inadequate funding for information literacy within this sector. She is of the view that public libraries have been forced to develop their own responses to the proclamations about information literacy, balancing between the responsibility for providing information literacy instruction programmes with their limited resources and the demands of the community (p. 280). Limited funding has resulted in public libraries' need to focus on certain aspects of information literacy rather than on the whole process. Examples provided by Harding (2008, p. 284) include:

- the investment of public libraries into information and communication technology and computer access and training, which aims at meeting the demands of clients for training in online searching;
- ad hoc 'teachable moments' where individual instruction moves from the teaching of basic access skills to more complex evaluation skills, and developing partnerships with:
  - schools and academic institutions, where public librarians are actively engaged with the provision of curriculum assistance and tailoring collections to suit students after school hour needs; and
  - securing funding to enable effective information literacy training of library staff and funding to provide community information literacy training.

Addressing information literacy from a Danish perspective, Skov (2004) suggests that part of the problem with information literacy provision in the public library sector, is the lack of a common language that describes information literacy. The term more commonly used in Denmark is 'informationskompetence', which describes 'user education and library instruction encompassing student learning and the pedagogical role of the librarian' (para 2). This lack of common language for information literacy (or 'informationskompetence'), results in many public libraries interpreting the term to include all traditional library activities such as library orientation, user education, user-librarian negotiation (reference) digital services as all inclusive of the information literacy concept. In this context teaching information literacy also becomes synonymous with information searching skills. Thus the power of the concept is reduced to a library-centric view (Skov, 2004). The author suggests public librarians are ill equipped to teach information literacy as a broad concept. This illustrates one of the tensions between educators and librarians in relation to information literacy education and highlights the public library's role as a supporting one. Skov (2004) suggests that:

> teaching students to become information literate is not done solely by teaching information searching, it requires a painstaking effort to teach critical thinking, formulation of research questions, analysis and evaluation of information. It is formal education's business to impart these competencies to students and the responsibility lies with teachers being the main stakeholders in the learning process (para 13).

However, a reality of public libraries not often mentioned is that they are open to school children long after teachers have left their classrooms. Consequently, information literacy education and supporting the school curriculum is an issue for these institutions, who must juggle the needs of a specific group in addition to the competing needs of many diverse interest groups within the community. Therefore, public libraries face a difficult task when it comes to the effective provision of information literacy within the community. The diverse nature, skills and needs of their constituent base; the limited recognition of the critical role that public libraries play supporting the community; a failure of governments to provide adequate financial support for information literacy programmes; and, the failure of peak library and education bodies to support public libraries in the development of information literacy programmes have resulted in an ad hoc approach to information literacy development for this sector. A number of other factors that affect the development of information literacy programmes in public libraries are listed by Harding (2008, pp. 274–294) as:

- lack of agreed standards, frameworks or guidelines that would provide a blueprint for public libraries;
- resources, such as staff, funding, space and facilities, which place limitations on what can be done within this sector;
- perceptions, attitudes and beliefs from staff about what information literacy is, including:
  - a lack of understanding and knowledge by public librarians as to what constitutes information literacy for this sector and what practices are the most important;

- valuing information (librarians need to accommodate the ways clients value information);
- public awareness of the public library as a provider of information literacy;
- support and acknowledgement of the public library's information literacy role by government, industry bodies; and
- nature of the public library (serves community demands).

Importantly, Harding (2008) also points out that public librarians are not perceived as having a teaching role, even though there is a general perception within the community and among peak organizations that public libraries *are* learning institutions. This is reflected and often reinforced in library and information science teaching programmes, where teaching skills are not routinely taught to librarians as part of their own professional education. Consequently, for this sector there is often an ad hoc approach to information literacy education and minimal promotion of the practice to the wider community.

Empirical research

As mentioned earlier, there are few studies of information literacy in public libraries. However, of these studies reported, some share a common range of issues. In particular, a lack of support for public libraries from other sectors, funding and, the librarian's perception about their role in supporting the information literacy education of their clients.

Research in Canada by Julien and Breu (2005) documented current information literacy instructional practices and also investigated public librarians' attitudes towards the delivery of information literacy programmes. The information and communication technology focus of this quantitative study was aligned with the Canadian government's imperative to ensure maximum connectivity for its citizens. Reporting on the first phase of the study, which examined the gap between government policy intent and the provision of information literacy services, the researchers observed:

- that information literacy was not a high priority within this sector, even though it is deemed by librarians to be important for all the community;
- that a small number of libraries are taking a large role in the development of information literacy skill development in the community;

- that there is perception that information literacy training is being imposed on this sector with little funded support to ensure success; and

- a strong injection of resources to support information literacy services is needed (e.g. dedicated funding, trained staff and training space).

Julien and Breu (2005, pp. 297–298)

The role of Canadian public libraries in developing information literacy skills (web-based) of community users was the basis of the second study by Julien and Hoffman (2008). Employing the ACRL definition, the authors understand information literacy to be a 'set of skills needed to find, retrieve, analyse and use information' (p. 24). The study explored the public use of the Internet, current training practices, users' opinions of their information literacy skills in using the Internet and the experiences of the staff. While the Canadian government has provided the information and communication technology infrastructure to roll out the Internet to public libraries across the nation, limited resources to provide information literacy training to the community have meant that policy objectives could not be fully met, i.e. the intention is to '… provide Canadians greater opportunities to develop the skills necessary to access online information' (p. 20).

The information literacy environment identified by Julien and Hoffman's (2008, pp. 33–39) study of Canadian public libraries highlights that:

- training remained a comparatively minor priority with little formal training given;

- clients are learning themselves and developing information literacy skills through experience and consulting with other people for advice and help rather than using formal training when offered by libraries;

- funding dedicated to the task of information literacy was lacking; and

- there was a lack of dedicated trained staff and space for training.

The authors found that there is a 'second level digital divide' emanating from a 'misplaced confidence many Canadians have in their ability to find, assess and appropriately use information' (p. 21). It is possible that time (alone) spent on the Internet might or might not develop information literacy skills 'more likely this experience develops confidence rather than actual skills' (p. 39). However, the authors observed the importance that information and communication technology training opportunities gave: '… some people the increased sense of community and of self-efficacy that accompanies Internet use might be strong starting point for the development of more sophisticated online skills (development training).' (Julien and Hoffman, 2008, p. 39).

The issue of transfer was also noted within this study. Reflecting on the lack of transfer of skills from formal information literacy education, the authors noted that: 'One interesting yet unsettling theme was the informal training provided to students at all levels, from grade school through to postsecondary, who apparently receive insufficient training in their educational contexts. This issue was noticeable at all the libraries visited' (Julien and Hoffman, 2008, p. 35). Similarly, the authors noted that: '… people are mostly training themselves, developing their information literacy skills through personal experience and seeking help from informal personal sources, such as friends and family, rather than through formal library training' (Julien and Hoffman, 2008, p. 39).

In this research, public librarians in Canada note that they are required to provide informal training to students who are not receiving it in a school setting. Again this point highlights the mismatch between the education and public sector about the adequacy of information literacy education for school children. The lack of collaboration between the education sector and the public library is of concern. In most cases it will be public librarians who are called in to pick up the deficit in information literacy training, primarily because of their greater accessibility. It also points to a greater need for library and information science courses to include some form of small group training in their curriculum.

Education for librarians is not a new issue. The information literacy perspectives of all types of librarians in Washington State were sought in the Bruce and Lampson (2002) study. It was intended that the implications gleaned from the views collected would then help determine the information literacy education needs for librarians. In this study the largest cohort were public librarians who: '… expressed the greatest need for support and training. Additionally, public librarians felt the most ill at ease in the teaching environment' (Bruce and Lampson, 2002, p. 101).

The type of information literacy support provided by public librarians tended to be 'one-on-one support for people with information needs … connecting information literacy service and instruction with the reference services of the library' (Bruce and Lampson, 2002, p. 92). However, librarians wanted to see more information literacy classes offered in the library supported by active promotion of current information literacy activities. They were aware that: 'Until and unless time, staffing and resources are allocated to support the development of a proactive program of information literacy within the institution, librarians indicated that reference staff will continue to respond to the need for information literacy in an ad-hoc, reactive fashion on an individual-by-individual basis.' (Bruce and Lampson, 2002, p. 102).

Hart (2006) has explored the relationship between the public library, and its readiness to undertake an instructional role in information literacy. The aim of this research was to investigate how ready public libraries in South Africa were to deliver expanded information literacy programmes. In particular, the study was interested in the delivery of information literacy to school students who used the public library, in a rural province, where only 18% of schools have libraries and as a consequence, support falls to the public library. In terms of 'readiness' the study aimed to identify the:

- levels of facilities and infrastructure needed for information literacy programme delivery, and

- willingness by librarians to take on an enhanced role in information literacy education.

The author envisaged that these two key elements were intertwined and central to the current information literacy environment in South African public libraries.

The library staff interviewed for this study had a narrow view of the public library's information literacy role and the staff's ability to describe information literacy and the search process suggested an incomplete understanding of information literacy. However, the author was optimistic that there was a 'dawning recognition that the public library has no choice but to intervene in pupils' information literacy education' (Hart, 2006, p. 60).

The second element that was found to be vital for the expansion of information literacy programmes was the existing facilities and infrastructure. Hart indicates that in South Africa there is a lack of physical facilities. In addition, the lasting effects of the apartheid system still impact on quality of service (Hart, 2006).

Given the intertwined nature of the two issues and the need for strategic change to take place, the study's 'fundamental' conclusion was that in order for cultural change to take place 'sustainable information literacy education in public libraries will depend on dynamic leadership and on a vision of a new model of the public library'. (Hart 2006, p. 60).

In 2001 the Information Literacy subgroup of the Library and Information Association of New Zealand Aotearoa (LIANZA) surveyed public libraries to identify the nature and extent of information literacy practices. The survey aimed to identify:

- the extent and range of formal and informal programmes provided by public libraries;
- the extent to which information literacy education programmes are formalized in planning and policy; and
- what public libraries consider they need to develop information literacy education.

Koning (2001, p. 170)

The areas to progress the information literacy agenda were identified as:

- increasing staff awareness of the importance of information literacy in their roles as librarians;
- developing and sharing planning documents;
- training (high level of need for skills in reference and e-resources, IT, information literacy and teaching);
- partnership development;
- government recognition of the role of libraries in information literacy development as being crucial to the knowledge/information society to progress information literacy education; and
- developing:
  - basic and advanced study skills for children and adults
  - study guides on 'hard' copy and online for sharing
  - basic computing skills training for the community
  - literacy and study skills for all levels of the library.

Koning (2001)

Partnerships with other institutions

Public libraries are uniquely placed to partner with other institutions for information literacy development, given the librarian's broad mandate of service offerings (Skov, 2004). Commenting on the Danish public library situation Skov (2004) notes that public libraries have a strong role as a support institution in information literacy partnerships with schools, not only for information literacy skill development but in developing critical thinking, question formulation and information evaluation in the children of the community. Skov (2004, para 14) wrote, 'If the concept of information literacy is taken to its fullest extent, the challenge of the public library is to get involved in the knowledge construction process of school children in collaboration with schoolteachers and school librarians'.

In describing an example from Denmark, Skov also highlights the outcomes of this partnership in terms of the development of shared values related to learning and student project work and a more collaborative approach between teachers and librarians where teachers are offered information searching courses. In return, librarians have been able to develop knowledge about new teaching methods. Citing the joint projects between public libraries and formal education in Århus, Denmark, Skov (2004, para 14) suggests that the collaboration and knowledge sharing by both groups has also produced a range of intangible results, such as 'an increased knowledge of how the library can support new teaching methods and assist students in their learning process, and a shared understanding of the concept of information literacy'.

In a national survey in New Zealand, Koning (2001) reports that partnerships were most often formed with schools (56% of public libraries). The example of schools is mirrored in the several examples given in Skov (2004). Other institutions where partnerships were identified were training institutions (30%) and community organizations (26%). Interestingly though, there is little mention of efforts to form partnerships with local businesses, although Koning (2001) notes that larger libraries were more likely to partner with these groups.

Need for national information policies and initiatives

In the same way that the agenda for information literacy in higher education needs to be supported and/or driven by university management and policy, it is also true of information literacy in the broader community. However, in the community context information literacy needs to be propelled by policy initiatives driven at the national level (Bundy, 2002; Candy, 2002; Correia, 2002). Such policies provide the support and impetus for the development of information literacy in various contexts, including libraries, community centres and museums, and to the professions. Candy (2002, p. 12) notes that:

> Despite Zurkowski's call as long ago as 1974 for national strategic approaches to the development of information literate students and

citizens, most governments have until recently been less than wholehearted in their commitment to this goal. In recent years, there has been a flurry of aspirational policies and national agendas about becoming information economies and learning societies, and even some tentative advocacy for information literacy.

Information literacy and lifelong learning are inextricably entwined and this strong connection is evident in the Prague Declaration and further developed in the Alexandria Proclamation. Candy's white paper for the Prague meeting of information literacy experts (2002) sets the agenda on this issue. He argues that:

> The first ... requirement (is) that people must have access to needed information; and the second is that they must be able to judge the quality of the information to which they are exposed. As a result, discourses about lifelong learning have become inextricably interwoven with, on the one hand, concerns about equitable access to information (much of which is in digital form) and, on the other hand, policies and practices designed to enhance the capacity to deal with large—often overwhelming—amounts of information (p. 13).

Aspirational information literacy: governance and civil society

Information literacy for an 'active, effective and responsible citizenship' is an area where there are a multitude of aspirational statements, but very little attention from researchers (Correia, 2002, p. 24). Citizens without good information literacy skills have limited access to information and as such strike barriers that prevent participation in their community. Ferrerio (in Garner, 2006, p. 45) wrote, 'Information Literacy is more than a sum of attributes, it is a process that facilitates social inclusion, through pedagogical mobilisation of interrelated content including knowledge, skills, attitudes and values of citizens.'

The importance of this issue is highlighted in the Alexandria Proclamation, where one particular group was dedicated to exploring the implications of information literacy for governance and citizenship. The aim of the group was to: '... empower people to actively participate in governance and citizenry and to control their own lives, respecting cultural diversity in both oral and digital societies as a public good.' (Garner, 2006, p. 18).

The target audience for the recommendations that emerged from the meeting was: 'political and civic leaders, NGOs, community groups, government agencies (national and international), international foundations, libraries, labour unions, educational institutions, business and industry, media.' (UNESCO, NFIL and IFLA, 2006, p. 18).

In a White Paper developed for the Prague meeting, Correia (2002) explores the dimensions and importance of information literacy for all members of the community. Correia (p. 4) states:

> In short, if citizenship is about making informed choices and decisions, about taking action, individually and as part of collective processes, to play a full part as active citizens and to be civically engaged through the exercise of moral responsibility, community involvement and exercise of their rights and responsibilities, then people need to acquire participatory skills. In parallel, they need to be information literate, at least at a basic level. They need the skills to enable them to locate, access, retrieve, evaluate, interpret and act on information, in order to identify, monitor and anticipate problems and communicate needs. They need to be able to exercise political, civil and social rights and responsibilities for self and others. Communication skills are also an essential element for an active and responsible citizenship, as people need to communicate to be able to express ideas and opinions with the confidence that they will be heard and taken into account.

Correia (2002) further suggests that effective citizenry requires that people are able to make practical use of information, not when engaged in formal educational settings but also in their work and everyday environments. In particular, information literacy provides the tools necessary for effective and informed decision making, enabling citizens to critically assess political environments, and to recognize 'misinformation, deception or disinformation' (pp. 15–16). In this regard Correia recognizes the power of information literacy and the ability of the phenomenon to improve an individual's body of knowledge (Correia, 2002).

Seeking the key concepts that underpin policy initiatives and competencies that will 'promote an information literate citizenry', Correia (2002, p. 13) researched the topic 'what are the information literacy competencies for an active, effective and responsible citizenship' (p. 12). Correia (p. 13) identified three broad conceptual categories.

(i) Education for citizenship (as a continuous process, both in the formal education system and in the informal adult education system for lifelong learning).

(ii) Creation of an information environment through the implementation of information policies with the emphasis on access and provision of quality information for citizenship.

(iii) Public and Civil Society Institutions as Information Intermediaries.

The Alexandria Proclamation (Garner, 2006, pp. 18–19) makes a number of recommendations relating to government and citizenship and urges national governments to create councils to promote an information culture. Other recommendations include the need to:

- develop lead agencies to consult with other stakeholders (e.g. education and information and communication technology);

- create programmes that will produce information literate people;

- develop information literacy standards in the workplace and business sectors; and

- address unemployment through information literacy education and to address the need for civics and citizenship education through information literacy programmes.

It is assumed that much of this work will fall to the public library sector but without the will and funding of governments then it is highly unlikely that these institutions will be able to convert information literacy ideals into reality.

Health information literacy

Health information literacy is a tangible and powerful concept for providing examples of information literacy in action, thus making it easier to communicate to the general public its value, whereas the abstract concept of information literacy is more difficult to promote (Wedgeworth, in Garner, 2006, p. 63). For example, Wedgeworth noted that 'people are motivated to know more about their health and the health of their families' (pp. 63–64). Developing good health information literacy programmes and strategies are vital for the empowerment of all individuals in all countries. A strong focus on information literacy in education sector programmes is vital if people are to become empowered in relation to health care and better able to make informed decisions not only about their own situations but contribute to improving the situations of others. There are a number reasons why health information literacy is vital. According to Candy (in Garner, 2006, p. 55) these are that:

- it is vital that all actors understand any documents, charts, records, dosages, treatments, etc., to ensure proper care and accurate diagnosis, treatment and instructions;
- everyone needs to understand the information needed about their own health;
- governments have a large responsibility—for both ideological and financial reasons;
- health is increasingly international in scope, with migration and refugees and air travel diseases that spread as fast as or faster than the information about the diseases;
- health and human services are a large and growing part of the economy with more and more potential for inter-sectoral collaboration such as between education, care providers, insurance companies, libraries, publishers and pharmaceutical companies;
- within health there is a long tradition of people helping each other (these traditions of self-help on the one hand and mutual support have become even more pronounced since the advent of the internet);
- information and communication technologies have a particular impact on the provision of health and human services ranging from e-health and telemedicine and integrated patient care records to patient networks;
- health information comes in a variety of forms and formats (photos, text, graphs, CDs, websites, etc.) and, thus, illustrates the multifaceted nature of information literacy—it is, therefore, a good test site for information literacy;
- health is so fundamental to the human condition.

There is a strong relationship 'between the lack of Health Information Literacy and poverty' (Wedgeworth, in Garner, 2006, p. 61). Much information is available on the Web; consequently, those lacking the technology and those with poor information literacy and information technology skills encounter deep barriers for access to quality health information. This in turn affects their ability to make informed decisions. The preamble in the Alexandria Proclamation provides the context to the Health and Human Services recommendations:

In the context of a universal commitment to enhanced quality of life, all citizens have a right to good health and to healthcare based on informed consent, which is reaffirmed and supported by this declaration. In support of this right, we reaffirm the entitlement of all citizens to access information that is relevant to their health and the health of their families and communities. In particular we refer to the necessary protection of the mother and the child as embodied in the Universal Declaration on Human Rights, to the rights of children to have access to information about health as enshrined in the United Nations Convention on the Rights of the Child (Article 26), and to the rights of all people to have sufficient information and understanding to give informed consent to treatment.

Garner (2006, p. 14)

In order to promote information literacy in this sector, Candy has argued that there needs to be greater clarity and precision about what information literacy means. I have (2005) argued that information literacy will mean different things according to the context in which it is practised. Candy makes the same point, and also suggests that information literacy is a contextual practice, consequently, what constitutes information literacy will be influenced by the discourse that shapes the setting. Therefore, in each domain, information literacy practises may exhibit some characteristics that are unique to the setting (e.g. a focus on information and communication technology, or on oral communication practices). In order to account for the variability in health information literacy, Candy suggests more co-ordination between national, regional and local approaches, which attempts to disseminate best practice, needs to be developed and supported. He points out that information literacy development in this area must recognize cultural difference. He also suggests that special attention should be paid to training healthcare professionals in information literacy education in order for these practices to be passed on and thus benefit and empower communities in respect to decision making related to their health (Candy, 2002, p. 57).

Putting a figure on the costs of poor health information literacy Wedgeworth (in Garner, 2006, p. 61) suggests that: '… there are estimates that in North America more than 75 billion dollars is wasted because people don't understand their physician's instructions and end up going to the emergency room. This has driven the American Medical Association to be actively involved in Health Information Literacy and the training of health care professionals'.

In the field of health it is easy to be misled into believing that the only issue is dissemination and access to information; evaluation and the use of information are critical aspects that are sometimes overlooked. Byrne, an Australian participant at the Alexandria meeting discussed the human costs of poor health information literacy that involve: '... misleading information, incorrect information and dangerous information—all of which makes Information Literacy more important in the field of health. The higher-level message we should be striving for is if you seek out information, and don't have the skills to evaluate it, you place your loved ones in jeopardy' (Byrne, in Garner, 2006, p. 65).

Apart from a number of aspirational statements alluding to the importance of information literacy practice in this sector, a number of recommendations were made in relation to health information literacy. These included:

- the development of integrated curriculum for all years of schooling and focused towards responsibility for health;
- the strengthening of partnerships with existing health organizations (e.g. World Health Organization (WHO), NGOs) and other public health organizations;
- the empowering of carers and patients through information literacy education, enabling them to ask questions and make informed decisions;
- advocacy for information literacy within the health profession;
- training of health professionals to improve their information literacy skills; and
- development of a best practice database to demonstrate quality information literacy programmes and initiatives.

Garner (2006, pp. 14–15)

Characteristics of information literacy in the public sector landscape

While the public sector is diverse and complex, the current perception of information literacy within this landscape is understood in specific ways— as a library-centric practice that focuses around information searching and the effective use of information and communication technology and library skills. This view also underpins a number of tensions and issues that exist in the debate within this sector, creating ambiguity about what information literacy is, what constitutes information literacy education and how the community should be supported (and by whom). In particular there is a need to reconcile the aspirational statements made by peak bodies relating to the importance of information literacy to all people. This relates to the need to provide education for librarians that will allow them to move away from the library-centric idea of information literacy and move towards a broader focus that includes training delivery. This requires not only advocacy by peak bodies to governments to obtain sustained funding, but also a commitment by library and information science educators to providing librarians with training specific to information literacy. This moves beyond the research process to include aspects of information literacy that are not based on print or information communication and technology literacy. Based on the current literature the landscape appears to exhibit the following characteristics:

- perceptions of information literacy and information literacy practice tend to follow library-centric models blending bibliographic instruction with a user education model—in this respect the concept of information literacy for this sector is more closely aligned with 'informationskompetence' found in Nordic countries;
- the lack of clear focus results in an inability to effectively advocate the importance of information literacy to funding bodies;
- the tendency to apply ad hoc approaches to information literacy education as a result of poor funding to the sector;
- focus towards a narrow skills education (e.g. information searching and information and communication technology orientation) rather than more complex features of information literacy, which would facilitate the lifelong learning agenda, as it is advocated by peak bodies;
- a high level of reflexivity about librarian ability (or lack of abilities) in information literacy training;
- it is driven by a tension that is created by aspirational statements attesting to the importance of information literacy to empowering citizens and lifelong learning—this tension results in public librarians feeling that the discourse of information literacy is being 'imposed' upon them with little understanding of the realities of practice within this sector.

Conclusions

Currently, there is a research lacuna into information literacy in the public sector. Of the research that has been conducted, themes centre on advocacy for information literacy as a prerequisite for lifelong learning. They also consider the tensions and difficulties faced by librarians in public libraries to support the learning of students who use the library outside school time, in addition to the diverse interests of the community. Conceptions of information literacy education appear to focus on the library-centric instructional models with a strong emphasis on searching for information and computer literacy.

References

ALIA. (2006). *Statement on information literacy for all Australians.* Australian Library and Information Association. Retrieved 13 October 2008 from http://www.alia.org.au/policies/information .literacy.html/.

Breivik, P. S. and Gee, E. (1989). *Information literacy; revolution in the library.* New York: Macmillan.

Brey-Casiano, C. A. (2006). From literate to information literate communities. *Public Library Quarterly*, 25(1/2), 181–190.

Bruce, H. and Lampson, M. (2002). Information professionals as agents for information literacy. *Education for Information*, 20, 81–106.

Bundy, A. (2002). Growing the community of the informed: information literacy: a global issue. *Australian Academic and Research Libraries*, 33(3), 125–134.

Candy, P. (2002). *Information literacy and lifelong learning,* White paper prepared for UNESCO, the US National Commission on Libraries and Information Science, and the National Forum on Information Literacy, for use at the *Information Literacy Meeting of Experts*, Prague, The Czech Republic. Retrieved on 25 September 2008 from http://74.11.214.110/libinter/infolitconf&meet/papers/candy-fullpaper.pdf/.

Correia, A. M. R. (2002). *Information literacy for an active and effective citizenship.* White paper prepared for UNESCO, the US National Commission on Libraries and Information Science, and the National Forum on Information Literacy, for use at the Information Literacy Meeting of Experts, July 2002, Prague, Czech Republic, retrieved

25 September 2008 http://74.11.214.110/libinter/infolitconf&meet/papers/correia-fullpaper.pdf/.

Garner, S. (2006). *High-level colloquium on information literacy and lifelong learning.* Bibliotheca Alexandrina, Alexandria, Egypt, November 6–9, 2005. Report of a Meeting Sponsored by the United Nations Educational, Scientific and Cultural Organization (UNESCO), National Forum on Information Literacy (NFIL) and the International Federation of Library Associations and Institutions (IFLA). Retrieved 13 January 2009, http://archive.ifla.org/III/wsis/High-Level-Colloquium .pdf/.

Hansen, J. N. (2004). The public libraries and information literacy in a Nordic perspective. *Scandinavian Public Library Quarterly*, 3, 31. Retrieved 8 January 2009, http://www.splq.info/issues/vol37_3/11.htm/.

Harding, J. N. (2008). Information literacy and the public library: We've talked the talk, but are we walking the walk? *Australian Library Journal*, 56, 48–62.

Hart, G. (2006). The information education readiness of public libraries in Mpumalanga Province (South Africa). *Libri*, 56, 48–62.

Julien, H. and Breu, R. D. (2005). Instructional practices in Canadian public libraries. *Library and Information Science Research*, 27(3), 281–301.

Julien, H. and Hoffman, C. (2008). Information literacy training in Canada's public libraries. *Library Quarterly*, 78(1), 19–41.

Koning, A. (2001). Information literacy in New Zealand. *APLIS*, 14(3), 159–164.

NCLIS, NFIL, and UNESCO. (2003). *The Prague Declaration. 'Towards an information literate society'*. Report on the Information literacy meeting of experts. http://portal.unesco.org/ci/en/files/19636/11228863531PragueDeclaration.pdf/PragueDeclaration.pdf/.

Ryynanen, M. (2002). *Information literacy, libraries and policy makers.* White paper prepared for UNESCO, the US National Commission on Libraries and Information Science, and the National Forum on Information Literacy, for use at the Information Literacy Meeting of Experts, Prague, The Czech Republic, retrieved 26 September 2008 from http://www.splq.info/issues/vol37_3/11.htm/.

Skov, A. (2004). Information literacy and the role of public libraries. *Scandinavian Public Library Quarterly*, 3(4–7) retrieved January 2009 from http://www.splq.info/issues/vol37_3/02.htm/.

Virkus, S. (2003). Information literacy in Europe: a literature review. *Information Research*, 8(4), 1–102.

Landscapes of information literacy

Introduction

By now it will be apparent that across the landscapes, information literacy is multifaceted, many layered, and more than just a set of skills to be mastered. This complexity is further compounded by diverse views about information literacy—what it is, how it should be researched and what are the most effective ways to teach the practice. In the tertiary education landscape, and here I include formal vocational training, there is on the one hand a strong and prevailing tendency for information literacy to be viewed as a competency and skills-based literacy, one that will produce a checklist of measurable and assessable information skills and attributes. On the other side of this landscape (and in opposition to the skills-based approach) another view clearly links information literacy with the different ways of interacting and experiencing information (Bruce *et al.*, 2007; Lupton, 2008).

In the workplace, our understanding of how information literacy contributes to practice and participation in working life is still emerging. However, the research that has been undertaken suggests that even though a skills-based view is prevalent, here too, other views and ways of thinking about information literacy are also emerging. These views contribute to a richer understanding of how workplace learning occurs and identify the socio-cultural dimensions that influence an experience with information and thus inform information literacy practice. This work is of particular relevance because it has the ability to inform and transform educational practice (Harris, 2008; Lloyd, 2006b; Hepworth and Smith, 2008). These alternative non-library-centric views highlight the collaborative nature of the workplace and its specific discourses and practices that shape the circumstances and conditions through which information literacy is made visible.

The most complex and difficult landscape to characterize is that of the public and community sectors, primarily because of the many settings and interests involved. Again, in this landscape further research is required. It appears, however, from the research that is available that a library-centric view of information literacy still prevails, which is reduced even further to focus on information literacy, as it is constituted through information searching and use of information and communication technology and computer literacy. In this sector, the perception of information literacy is underpinned with: (1) tensions relating to the role of the public library as a centre for learning that is often found in many peak bodies' aspirational documents; (2) a high level of reflexivity by librarians in this sector about their ability to undertake the teaching of information literacy; and (3) questions from other stakeholder groups (e.g. teachers) about whether this is really the public librarians' role.

This chapter will explore further the concept of an information literacy landscape that was first introduced in Chapter 2. It will be used to explain complexities of information literacy by illustrating its holistic and collaborative nature. A central thesis of this book is that as researchers, educators and practitioners we need to understand how information literacy practices occur in other contexts so that our own pedagogical practice prepares our users for the transition from one landscape to another.

Information literacy landscapes: a general overview

Physical landscapes are structured and characterized by different topographies, climates and complex ecologies. Depending on how a person interacts and experiences them, these landscapes can be perceived and subsequently interpreted in many different ways. Every landscape has a distinctive shape and features that are specific to it. The shape of the landscape is influenced over time by many interrelated processes, such as climate, erosion, deposition, tectonic forces or volcanic activity. All these activities in turn shape the complex ecologies that exist within the landscape and provide the conditions for the existence of living things.

Similarly within human contexts, discourse, social order, and an array of practices structure and shape the information landscape, giving it a specific character and agreed ways of performance. The structuring of an information landscape enables access to certain types of information while constraining the influence of other sources. Inhabiting a landscape, allows members to engage with information and to learn about how the site is heritaged, its social formation and arrangements, to gain knowledge about its patterns and cycles and to develop subjective positions in relation to it (e.g. librarian, teacher librarian, public librarian). Over time, people learn to read their landscape by developing specific and appropriate information practices, often embedded within other practices and skills that allow them to interrogate it, and to use its resources. Through information practices they develop 'understanding and intelligibility' (Schatzki, 1996, p. 12), which leads to a shared sense of meaning, of place and identity. They develop ways of talking about the landscape, of passing on its history, traditions and practices. Over time certain people become in essence, indigenous to particular types of landscapes, constructing their own identities in relation to place. By situating themselves within the landscape, people engage and interact with its complexity, developing appropriate practices, strategies and skills that will enable them to mine the richness of the environment. People also learn to protect their landscape and its traditions, by creating barriers that can make it difficult for outsiders to enter.

All information landscapes are constructed and grounded through collaborative practice and maintained through membership. Consequently, they are socially produced and while they may appear less tangible than a physical landscape, the act of being in it is just as real. Like a physical landscape, an information landscape can have a varied topography, and can be inhabited by a number of groups who while sharing a central language and narrative have specific information and knowledge that make them unique subcommunities.

When we first engage with an information landscape (through an occupation, education or circumstance, i.e. health or even sport) we need to learn about it, to understand the powerful forces that shape its structures and influence its flow. We need to develop practices that will allow us to map its resources, to interpret its language and nuances and to understand the social, historical, political and economic trajectory and imperatives that have shaped it along with the practices, including the information practices, and skills that are sanctioned within it. As part of this we also need to understand what practices, skills and knowledge must be developed to equip us as we journey through the landscape.

For the less well travelled, a landscape may seem unfamiliar, formidable, difficult to traverse, inhospitable, and ultimately difficult to know. Without assistance it may be easy to get lost along the paths or within nodes, or go beyond the edges of the landscape. However, for those with appropriate knowledge and understanding of how to read the landscape and with the help of some guides and landmarks, the terrain may take on a different character and become *knowable* (Lloyd, 2006b).

Because of the varied nature of landscapes, different skills, practices and affordances are required to make the information and knowledge within them accessible. In some cases where learning is formal and structured, the application of these skills requires a good deal of specific conceptual knowledge (*know-why* or propositional knowledge). At times and where learning may be informal and unstructured, the skills required might be drawn from embodied experience (*know-how* or practical knowledge). While at other times a combination will be required. The types of skills, practices and affordances that are valued within a landscape will be underpinned by the nature of the discourse that gives it character and influences the methods used to explore it (Lloyd, 2006b).

Information landscapes are not solitary places, but are full of other people who are connected through the same context. We recognize their membership because they tend to speak a similar language to us, and to share a similar understanding about the nature of the landscape and the practices that constitute it. To do this they need to develop an intersubjective understanding of what constitutes information and what information is recognized by the group as making a difference (Bateson, 1972). Our culturally adapted way of life depends on negotiation, contestation and agreement in order to develop shared meanings, shared concepts, and on the shared modes of discourse for negotiating difference in meanings and interpretation (Schwandt, 2003). Interacting with, and attending to, information in uniform ways enables the building of shared focus. It also establishes co-presence and permits the construction of mutually recognizable identities (e.g. as a student, a nurse, a librarian, a welder or a painter) and later on, our transformation to a collective identity within a professional workplace group.

However, when we first engage with our information landscapes we do so as novices or newcomers and others recognize us within the landscape as such. Over time information is used to draw us into a collective practice from the boundary to which we have been brought by our training or education (Lave and Wenger, 1991). Consequently when we first enter the landscape we need some kind of map, and this can be provided by preparatory education and training.

Over time, as we journey through the landscape, establish ourselves within it and develop our expertise, we undergo a transition, from being newcomers to becoming 'old timers' (Lave and Wenger, 1991). 'Old timers' are fully engaged with the landscape and because of their expert knowledge are able to move outside it, to create distributed networks in their search for salient information. Information that is drawn from distributed networks can then be used to further enhance and deepen their own practice and the practices of others within their community. This process of engaging with information, and developing the skills and competencies that facilitate engagement, also shapes our identities, which are produced and reproduced as we accumulate skills and knowledge. Acting as information guides, the members of the group will guide newcomers through the landscape providing them with the scaffolding required to understand which sources of information are legitimized and which ways of knowing sanctioned. Over time and with the help of our information guides, we find that the map of our information environment becomes more familiar, and we are able to read the changes and nuances of the landscape. In effect we become indigenous to it and the map we initially used will no longer be required.

However, engaging with an information landscape and learning to read and interpret it, can be problematic. Information landscapes can be closed to outsiders and only fully accessible to those whose membership is recognized. The creation of epistemic barriers can affect the information flow with a landscape, creating small communities with vested interests.

In summary, as a collaborative construction, all information landscapes are prefigured by historical, political, material and economic dimensions. These dimensions have been laid down over time and *sediment* as knowledge features that are shaped and reshaped through collaborative participation. When people connect to a landscape they connect with sources of information through a range of practices, all of which are sanctioned by the community. In connecting with members, and practices, the newcomer also connects with information that may be socially nuanced and embodied as a result of practical experience, or textual, relating to the codified rules and regulations that explicate the community's identity to the world. Creating this connection enables the newcomer to develop their identity within this community and to gain a sense of place. Over time these meanings are reproduced as experience of the landscape and the information within it deepens.

By using this analogy of landscape and how people come to know place and space, I hope to convey some of the complexities we face when trying to understand information literacy as a holistic socio-cultural practice and how this practice is manifest in a particular landscape.

Features of information literacy in the educational, workplace and community landscapes

Education settings

Unlike the workplace and community landscapes, information literacy in the education sector has been the most explored and analysed because of the boundedness of this landscape, which neatly divides the sectors into primary, secondary and tertiary. An artefact of this boundedness is that the conception of what information literacy is and how it is defined have become enmeshed with the discourse of educational practice and therefore fixed in the minds of most educators and librarians who practise in this setting.

In this landscape information literacy is strongly aligned with Western educational practices (i.e. a rationalist perspective) that emphasizes written word cultures and associated practices. The nature of Western education emphasizes an individual pursuit, and is underpinned by a positivist epistemology of 'single physical and social realities, or "worlds", separate from the student and accessible through language' (Kapitzke, 2003, p. 40). In this landscape, information is understood as objective, factual and discoverable (Kapitzke, 2003; Kirk, 2004). It is also where the ability to acquire, assimilate and apply information is assessable through some form of measurement, where skills are observable and can be benchmarked against established criteria and standards. This may seem a fairly pared down statement but it does not account for the many philosophies of education and pedagogies that influence ways of teaching and learning. However, the basic point is that education is shaped by a dualism that favours the mind over the body and therefore learning is understood as a mentalistic affair (Kapitzke, 2003; Lloyd, 2003).

Consequently, in educational settings, the information landscape is dominated by an epistemic modality, constructed through disciplinary understandings, where information is objective and sanctioned through external written sources of information that is made accessible by increasing reliance on digitized sources and technology. Information literacy as an information practice is often viewed in relation to digital and computer literacy and others skills that are closely associated to library literacy, in particular, information searching skills, evaluating information and higher order skills such as critical thinking about content.

There appears to be a fixed notion about what information literacy is in this landscape and this is largely influenced by the prevailing cognitive and/or epistemic paradigm coupled with the library-centric idea that information literacy is made visible through the systematic steps of the research process. Here the emphasis is on developing skills and competencies in order to access and evaluate information, to think about information and to demonstrate and document the process of that thinking, taking into account the ethical considerations of information access and use. Consequently, information literacy is understood as a discrete set of skills that is generic and transferable to aspects of everyday life (Lloyd, 2005).

The language of information literacy in an educational landscape, including a vocation training setting, shapes information literacy as a competency or skills-based literacy, primarily because of the Cartesian view (dualism), in which the mind is privileged over the body. This view favours conceptual *know-that* or propositional knowledge and influences cognitive or behavioural approaches to information literacy. Competency in this setting is therefore understood in terms of the knowledge, skills, abilities and attitudes that are displayed in context (Hager and Smith, 2004). If we refer to the information literacy standards we can see a competency-based understanding of information literacy at work (Association of College and Research Libraries (ACRL), 2000; Bundy, 2004a). The standards and guidelines prescribe and describe the knowledge, skills, abilities and attributes of an information literate person from an education/library perspective. When information literacy is framed through a cognitivist or behavioural lens, we should be able to measure information literacy competency and traits, through student restatement and replication. An underlying assumption of this approach is that information skills are generic and, therefore, transferable.

As the context in which these skills are being taught is preparatory, there is therefore an assumption that information literacy knowledge, skills that are learnt and attributes that are established through this learning will prepare students for the next stages of their lives, either through further education or work. All of this suggests that most models of information literacy, while arguing for the embeddedness of information literacy, are probably best thought of as front end models in which the information literacy process is taught as generically as possible in the belief that these skills will transfer from one information landscape to the next. As we saw in Chapters 4 and 5, this process is being questioned in the workplace and by public sector librarians.

Workplace landscape settings

The characteristics of information literacy in a post-Fordist workplace are less systematic, more complex and less measurable than they are for the education landscape. By nature, workplaces are complex, messy places where information and knowledge are highly contested. Becoming information literate is not an individual process in this context. Rather it is a holistic and collaborative process that requires practitioners to be reflective and reflexive, to develop skills and competencies that are relative and framed by the intersubjective understanding of which information, knowledge and practices are sanctioned and those which are not.

In this setting, when information literacy is viewed from a library-centric perspective, it is framed by the development of information skills, as librarians understand them. This approach does not take into account that becoming informed about the sources of information is more than a process of applying information skills to facilitate engagement with formal written sources of information. It is also a process of engaging with the social narrative and knowledge of the collective and corporeal sites that produce the embodied sources of information and knowledge. In this respect the nature of information literacy is best understood as a practice that is culturally shaped and one that reflects the situated nature of interaction between people engaged in a common endeavour.

It is from this workplace setting that another view of competence has also been framed, one that emphasizes the collective power of learning and draws from the work of practice theorists discussed in Chapter 2 of this book. In this more holistic view, competence is constructed and therefore relational (Beckett and Hager, 2002; Hager and Smith, 2004). This suggests that in order to understand information literacy as a competence, or even a meta-competence, as I suggested in 2003 (Lloyd, 2003) we need to understand it as a situated practice, one that is shaped by cultural determinants (e.g. values, beliefs, rituals and conventions) which are specific to the setting and prefigure the practices within it, including information practice and skill. In higher education settings, for example, value is placed on the written word and the verification of source veracity through a systematic evaluation of authority. In contrast to this, in the emergency services studies described in Chapter 4, value as a cultural determinant is placed on the tacitly disseminated embodied knowledge. This is judged through observation of other workers' practice (doing) and through the socially sanctioned and valued story telling (sayings) as a way of imparting embodied know-how and reinforcing cultural consensus.

This suggests that in a workplace landscape, information literacy is more than just the development of generic behaviour, skills and cognitive processes in an individual and something that can be transferred from one setting to the next. Competence is situated within the social settings in which a person enters and operates. Sandberg (2000, p. 55) suggests that 'although an individual's competency is central in performing an organization's tasks, it is above all in the interaction with others that the task can be performed in an acceptable way'.

Therefore, it is the collective that defines and determines which types of knowledge, skills and attributes are appropriate for the performance of context-specific practices. This determination will be influenced by the types of information modalities deemed important for practice and performance within a setting, with which a person must connect. Consequently in this view of competence, the skills are grounded in the practice and performance rather than within the person, and it is by engaging with the practice that a person becomes competent.

By adopting this more holistic view of competence we can take into account other forms of learning. In particular, the embodied practical understandings that are brought to the forefront when we think about workplace learning, one that is often more organic than the structured formalized learning that occurs in preparatory training contexts. This type of organic learning often goes beyond the technical, but focuses on learning to be part of a team, situated problem-solving and planning and most importantly the construction of new knowledge that is often brought about by practice understandings and reflection on action (praxis).

The collective view allows us to question the focus on information skills. The idea of information literacy as a generic competency with a set of transferable skills assumes that information skills exist as a separate and distinct competence. This view fails to acknowledge the importance of the context and its actors and the role each play in valuing, maintaining and sanctioning specific competency and skills. The ability to develop strong information-seeking skills is highly valued as part of the reference process by librarians in the education sector. However, in the workplace, the ability to learn effective information-seeking skills will depend on the value that is placed on this activity by the seeker in relation to the overall task of which information seeking is a part. Consequently, any argument about skill development must recognize that what constitutes a *skill* is a construction that is validated by the field in which the skill is practised.

Community landscape

The aspirational discourse constructed by the peak bodies for information literacy has created a landscape that is unmatched by funding that would enable information literacy to be effectively promoted or to develop programmes at community levels in order to meet the needs for learning throughout life. In this landscape the narrative focuses on information literacy as an empowering practice, a core literacy and prerequisite for lifelong learning, the key to economic success and a basic human right in a digital world (Garner, 2006). In this respect the community landscape is without doubt the most important; however, it is also the most contested and is marked by a difficulty in articulating information literacy beyond the library-centric information skills approach. This approach reflects the search process but fails to account for other aspects of information literacy, in particular, evaluation and critical thinking around information. It also assumes that information and communication technology is the dominant tool of the information literate practitioner. Across all landscapes the perception that information literacy equates to developing good information and communication technology and digital information literacy skills has also come into question. Bundy (2004b, p. 4) argues that this has resulted in a misjudgement that the 'key educational issue and investment of the information age is information technology'. While information technology is an important feature and developing information technology skills are critical to effective socio-technical practice, they are not the *sum* of information literacy practice. It does not take into account other sources and ways of knowing that may better reflect how information literacy actually occurs in community-based settings. This is not to say that information and communication technologies and information skills are not important, they are critically important, but they do not constitute the sum of information literacy practice, nor do they represent the needs of all groups within a community. In communities with a strong oral tradition and/or with limited resources, information and communication technology may not play a major part in information literacy. Information literacy practice will therefore take on a different form, and as a consequence, educational programmes will need to be developed that focus more on communication and critical thinking around other forms of information access and dissemination (Catts and Lau 2008).

Noteworthy in the public sector, is the high level of reflexivity that exists among librarians about their own teaching and pedagogical skills, or lack thereof. In addition, librarians in this sector recognize that information literacy has been thrust upon them, with little empirical evidence (apart from aspirational statements) that might provide guidelines or training for the development of best practice.

Contesting information literacy in the landscape

Research that is emerging from workplace and community landscapes has begun to contest the conception of information literacy particularly in relation to the prevailing view of it as a skills-based literacy and a library-centric view of information literacy education by librarians. This emerging level of questioning is critical to understanding it, and altering the discourse, which until recently has narrated information literacy and the process of becoming information literate as a largely unproblematic activity.

Bundy (2004b), who describes information literacy as a 'mosaic of attitudes, understandings, capabilities and knowledge' (p. 1), has attempted to dispel a number of myths that have led to contested understandings and practices in relation to information literacy. This author argues that an important characteristic that defines and distinguishes information literacy from information skills is the individual's recognition of the need for information. He suggests that this must be taught as part of information literacy programmes in order to develop a citizenry who can recognize their own needs for information and have the ability to become informed. While this may be appropriate in the education sector, evidence grounded in workplace research indicates that recognizing the need for information is often not an independent or even conscious activity. Information needs are *often* defined for employees in the form of directions from a supervisor to undertake a task (Hepworth and Smith, 2008). Similarly, in the fire-fighting study (Lloyd, 2006a), information gaps of novices were recognized by more experienced practitioners.

Equally, the library-centric idea that information literacy is primarily about teaching information skills, which reflect the skills required in the research process, has also been challenged by research emerging from the workplace, where the focus is on information literacy as a collaborative information practice. The perception that students enter high school, the workplace or even the community as information literate individuals has been recognized and contested across all landscapes as was discussed in Chapter 4. In the public library sector the lack of a range of information literacy-related skills has been identified (Harding, 2008). In the workplace the ability to effectively prepare a student to enter the workplace *work ready* has also been questioned.

Conclusions

When an individual engages in information literacy practice they are not simply engaging with formal modes of learning and associated skills. They are simultaneously engaging with a social world that is shaped by specific discourses and discursive practices, which affects the ways in which information is understood, shared and sanctioned.

The broad spectrum of information literacy that I have described in the last few chapters illustrates that the practice can be conceptualized and operationalized in a number of different ways. This has led to different, and often contested, understandings of what information literacy is and what elements constitute the practice and activities of information literacy. It also illustrates that at the present moment, there is no general theory of information literacy in the sense that Socrates, Kant or Descartes argue for, because as we have seen, there is great variation in the way information literacy manifests. This variation in itself precludes universal theorization, in the positivist sense, because to be thought of as *theory* requires a comprehensive account for all domain activity and clearly not all domains and not all activities are the same. The approach in this book departs from a positivist framework and adopts a constructionist approach; therefore, theory is understood as a general and abstract account of information literacy as it is understood and described within each of the landscapes rather than being characteristic of all three. For this to occur the research gaps for information literacy in the workplace and community contexts will need to be filled thus enabling contested views of information literacy practice to be examined and reconciled.

Having said that, I will propose in the next chapter an *architecture* for developing information literacy theory that takes into account a number of dimensions that may act as a foundational step towards theorization as more research into the complexities of the phenomenon is undertaken.

References

Association of College and Research Libraries (ACRL). (2000). Information literacy competency standards for higher education [Electronic Version]. Retrieved 10 September 2008 from http://www .ala.org/ala/mgrps/divs/acrl/standards/informationliteracycompetency.cfm.

Bateson, G. (1972). *Steps to an ecology of the mind.* San Francisco, CA: Jason Aronson Inc.

Beckett, D. and Hager, P. (2002). *Life, work and learning: practice in postmodernity.* London: Routledge.

Bruce, C., Edwards, S. and Lupton, M. (2007). Six frames for information literacy education: a conceptual framework for interpreting the relationship between theory and practice. In S. Andretta (Ed.), *Change and challenge: information literacy for the 21st century* (pp. 37–58). Blackwood, SA: Auslib Press.

Bundy, A. (2004a). *Australian and New Zealand information literacy framework: principles, standards and practice* (2nd ed.): Australian and New Zealand Institute for Information Literacy. Retrieved 28 September 2008 from http://www.anziil.org/resources/Info%20lit% 202nd%20edition.pdf/.

Bundy, A. (2004b). Zeitgeist: information literacy and educational change. In *The 4th Frankfurt Scientific Symposium.* Retrieved November 30 2008 http://www.library.unisa.edu.au/about/papers/ zeitgeist-info-lit.pdf/.

Catts, R. and Lau, J. (2008). *UNESCO. Information for all programme (IFAP). Towards information literacy indicators.* France: UNESCO. Retrieved 30 November 2008 from http://unesdoc.unesco.org/images/ 0015/001587/158723e.pdf/.

Garner, S. (2006). Report of a Meeting Sponsored by the United Nations Educational, Scientific and Cultural Organization (UNESCO), National Forum on Information Literacy (NFIL) and the International Federation of Library Associations and Institutions (IFLA). Retrieved 30 November 2008 http://archive.ifla.org/III/wsis/High-Level-Colloquium.pdf/.

Hager, P. and Smith, E. (2004). The inescapability of significant contextual learning in work performance. *London Review of Education,* 2(1), 33–46.

Harding, J. N. (2008). Information literacy and the public library: We've talked the talk, but are we walking the walk? *Australian Library Journal,* 56, 48–62.

Harris, B. (2008). Communities as necessity in information literacy development: challenging standards. *Journal of Academic Librarianship,* 34(3), 248–255.

Hepworth, M. and Smith, M. (2008). Workplace information literacy for administrative staff in higher education. *Australian Library Journal*, 57(3), 212–236.

Kapitzke, S. (2003). Information literacy: a positivist epistemology and politics of outformation. *Educational Theory*, 53(1), 37–53.

Kirk, J. (2004). Tumble dryers and juggernauts: information-use processes in organizations. In P. A. Danaher, C. McPherson, F. Nouwens and D. Orr (Eds), *Lifelong learning: Whose responsibility and what is your contribution?* Proceedings of the 3rd international lifelong learning conference (pp. 192–197). Yeppoon, Queensland Australia, 13–16 June. Rockhampton: Central Queensland University Press.

Lave, J. and Wenger, E. (1991). *Situated learning: legitimate peripheral participation*. New York: Cambridge University Press.

Lloyd, A. (2003). Information literacy: the metacompetency of the knowledge economy; an exploratory paper. *Journal of Librarianship and Information Science*, 35(2), 87–92.

Lloyd, A. (2005). Information literacy; different contexts, different concepts, different truths? *Journal of Librarianship and Information Science*, 37(2), 82–88.

Lloyd, A. (2006a). Drawing from others; ways of knowing about information literacy performance. In D. Orr, F. Nouwens, C. McPherson, R. E. Harreveld, and P. A. Danaher (Eds), *Lifelong learning: partners, pathways and pedagogies*. Keynote and refereed papers from the 4th international lifelong learning conference (pp. 182–192). Rockhampton: Central Queensland University Press.

Lloyd, A. (2006b). Information literacy landscapes: an emerging picture. *Journal of Documentation*, 62(5), 570–583.

Lupton, M. (2008). *Information literacy and learning*. Unpublished PhD, Queensland University of Technology.

Sandberg, J. (2000). Competence—the basis for a smart workforce. In R. Gergen and C. Lankshear (Eds), *Training for a smart workforce* (pp. 47–72). London: Routledge.

Schatzki, T. (1996). *Social practices: A Wittgensteinian approach to human activity and the social*. Cambridge: Cambridge University Press.

Schwandt, T. (2003). Three epistemological stances for qualitative inquiry: interpretivisim, hermeneutics and social constructionism. In *Handbook of Qualitative Research* (2nd ed., pp. 189–213). Thousand Oaks, CA: Sage Publications.

7

A conceptual architecture for information literacy practice

Introduction

This chapter will introduce a conceptual architecture for information literacy and present the critical features that contribute to our understanding of how information literacy practice manifests in different contexts. My intention here is to present a number of sensitizing concepts that I hope will encourage researchers and practitioners to reflect on their understanding of information literacy. To think about information literacy holistically, as a socio-cultural practice suggests that we need to focus not only on the skills of information literacy, but also to consider how the practice allows intelligibility and understanding of the information landscape to occur. This means that we need to understand information literacy as a collaborative information practice that is inherent in all other practices. Information literacy is a practice that allows us to understand the setting, and how it orders and operationalizes social life, including information and information practices, within it.

To understand how a person becomes information literate requires us to account for more than the acquisition of skills related to information searching or to the student research process. These are only one side of the information literacy equation. The other side is the ability to develop a deep understanding of the complexity of the information experience and to recognize what information is valued and how a community constructs knowledge. It also requires an account of the tensions within a setting that enable or constrain access to information. All information landscapes are socially constituted; therefore, being information literate requires that people are able to understand the information affordances that are furnished by others and by the socio-technical and material practices that are part of the landscapes' character. Becoming information literate requires skills beyond those we currently ascribe to the practice in educational circles and may include some that are not taught as part of a library-centric information literacy practice.

That is not to say that information skills are not an important feature of information literacy, they are. However, rather than impose a library-centric view on to other landscapes about what information activities skills are required, we should make attempts to understand what skills and activities are sanctioned by the setting as making an appropriate contribution to practice. To do this we have to understand how the various features of information literacy practice (i.e. activities, skills and process) fit together as a situated practice, one that is constructed according to sayings and doings of the setting that act to enable ways of knowing while constraining others.

Information literacy is not visible by itself; it is a meta-practice that is entwined with the actions of other practices through which people connect to sources of information within their landscape. As we have seen in the previous chapters of this book, information landscapes are complex webs of information, some of it codified and explicit, some of it social and tacit and some physical and embodied. The discourses of the community will produce particular ways of knowing which give the landscape its unique and recognizable features. Therefore, from a socio-cultural perspective information is always situated, nuanced and laced with particular sayings and doings that enable or constrain the practices of the setting. These prefigurements, i.e. how the environment enables and or constrains activity, by qualifying possible paths of action (Schatzki, 2002), influence the way information literacy manifests as socio-cultural practice and can be conceptualized in an architecture for information literacy. This architecture is not intended to be prescriptive but is indicative of the germane elements that influence the manifestation of information literacy and are present in all settings.

Conceptualizing an architecture for information literacy

Wenger (1998) has articulated the concept of architecture in relation to learning, and more recently Kemmis and Grootenboer (2008) have described it in relation to practice. It is a particularly useful way to conceptualize information literacy from a research and pedagogical perspective because it can illustrate the critical features that influence information literacy as a situated and collaborative practice. This is not to say that information literacy is generic, rather it points to a number of common elements that together constitute the features that influence the development of information literacy within a setting. In the context of a setting, these *features* will be overlaid with activities and skills that operationalize information literacy practice within a specific setting.

Wenger (1998) introduces the idea that learning is produced through conceptual architectures that exist on many levels and that 'lay down the general elements of design' (p. 230). This is particularly useful when thinking about information literacy as multifaceted and complex. Therefore to reveal and account for the complexity and thus inform our own practices, it becomes necessary to strip bare the structure that includes our own assumptions about what information and knowledge are.

Kemmis and Grootenboer (2008) take up this idea of architectures to develop the concept of practice architectures. They extend the concept further (p. 57) by suggesting that:

> organizations, institutions and settings, and the people in them, create *practice architectures* which prefigure practices, enabling them and constraining particular kinds of sayings, doings, and relatings, among people within them and in relation to others outside them. The way these practice architectures are constructed shapes practice in its cultural-discursive, social-political and material economic dimensions, giving substance and form to what is and can be actually said and done by, with and for whom.

The point these authors are making is that people *construct* these architectures by shaping and designing them to reflect the conduct and content of other practices in situ. Therefore, and as we have seen in previous chapters, workplaces will reflect particular historical, social, cultural, political and economic arrangements that in turn shape, enable or constrain the practices within them. While in education there will be a different set of arrangements that will reflect a different trajectory and formations that have been constructed over time.

Revisiting the practice perspective for information literacy

As we discussed in Chapter 2, framing the information landscape through a practice perspective allows us to see that each information landscape or site is shaped by the nature of information and by the relationship between people and information. It is this relationship that creates site knowledge and influences specific ways of knowing within the landscape. Just as each topography has its particular defining characteristics that shape the surrounding landscape, so too does information reflect the landscape of particular settings.

The first step in conceptualizing an architecture for information literacy is to recognize the ontological and epistemological arrangements that help position the researcher or practitioner in terms of how we think about and understand reality. An ontological understanding of information literacy may be described as a way of knowing *about what there is* (the constructed realities of a context) in an information landscape or the nature of reality (Lincoln and Guba, 2003). If we accept that information literacy is a practice that leads to a way of knowing and that an information literate person is a *knowing user of information*, then we can turn our attention to focusing on epistemological questions related to *what there is* (i.e. social, physical and textual sites of knowledge) and *how we come to know*. Understanding these elements puts us in a position to suggest how to facilitate information literacy practices that will then allow us to know these sites of knowledge.

As I indicated in Chapter 2, my approach to information literacy draws from socio-cultural perspectives and practice theory. This means that my view about the nature of reality (my ontology) is influenced by an understanding that there are multiple realities that influence the nature of knowledge and understanding. From this perspective, information and knowledge are understood as relational and constructed through engagement with discourse and objects in situ. This in turn produces between members who share the same intersubjective space, a web of shared understandings about place, identity and performance. The shared understandings are manifest and operationalized through site-specific practices, including information practice.

My epistemological approach, *how we come to know*, is formed through this site ontology (Schatzki, 2002). Consequently, we come to know through constructing meaning in negotiation with other people, through practices that are situated and shaped over time by social, cultural, economic and material arrangements that shape certain types of action (in addition to enabling or constraining them) and are revealed through the 'sayings and doings' of people as they participate in a setting (Schatzki, 2002; Kemmis and Grootenboer, 2008).

Consequently, and to rephrase Chapter 2, when I think about information literacy as a socio-cultural practice, I do so from a practice perspective that frames information and knowledge as being relational to a social site. Meaning making is emphasized as a collaborative process occurring in situ, leading to the production and reproduction of identity, to ways of interacting and to *ways of knowing*. Therefore, an understanding of information literacy practice also requires us to understand the information experiences of embodied performance, in addition to the abstract and reified constructions of a particular site. Understanding information literacy as a holistic practice therefore requires us to account not only for the activities and skills commonly ascribed to information literacy but also to the socio-cultural dimensions within the site, through which these skills and activities are enabled.

An emerging architecture for information literacy practice

In considering a conceptual architecture for information literacy, one that provides a basic design of sensitizing concepts for research and pedagogical development, a number of broad features must be taken into account. These features are introduced here, as *context*, which influences *discourse* and *information modality*. These in turn influence the *affordances* that constitute information literacy as socio-cultural information practice. The way these features emerge will depend on how they are sanctioned within context. Each will be described later in this chapter. Accounting for these features allows us to understand how information literacy is enabled and experienced as a dispersed practice (Schatzki, 2002). Dispersed practices flow within all areas of social life and are embedded in other integrated practices (e.g. teaching, working, library or learning practices). Integrated practices are in turn shaped and situated by culturally discursive, political and material arrangements (Schatzki, 2002). The architecture should also allow us to consider how information is enabled and constrained.

Concepts for theorizing information literacy architecture in the landscape model

The structure and organization of the landscape affords a range of opportunities for people to engage with the sources of information and sites of knowledge that have created their unique shape and character. There are a number of key features that must first be explored. Like geographic landscapes, information landscapes are shaped and modified by dominating features, these in turn affect the shape of other features within it.

Context matters

Context is woven and shaped by history, culture, norms, values, practices and tools (Hager and Smith, 2004). These dimensions are artefacts of people's interaction over time and consequently they influence the prefigurement of the practices that are enacted within any particular context (Schatzki, 2002). Therefore, context can be said to surround, influence, enable and constrain the practices, activities and ultimately the performance of people in situ (Schatzki, 2002). As researchers and practitioners we need to understand how a context or setting has been shaped by internal and external influences in order to recognize what it means to be an information literate person in a particular space. We also need to be aware of what activities within information literacy practice (i.e. other information practices, behaviours and skills) need to be operationalized in order to achieve a state of being information literate.

I am emphasizing a point here—that *context matters*! Consequently, any exploration or statement about information literacy has to include an account of context. It cannot be excluded or backgrounded when thinking about the information experience because it provides insights for researchers and practitioners into the landscape and clues to its shape and character. This in turn enables us to understand how information literacy is experienced and the activities, including skills, of information literacy are perceived.

Why context matters

This leads us back to the point that context matters and highlights the importance of understanding the setting and situations through which information literacy is practised and from which research and pedagogy will emerge. In discussing the idea of context, Brenda Dervin (1996, p. 32) suggests that 'context is something you swim in like a fish. You are in it, it is in you'. Dervin is right in suggesting this; we are a product of our contexts and at the same time are producers, shapers and interpreters of it. Context is constructed over time and has social, political, and economic trajectories that sanction some practices and process and exclude or contest others. Therefore, to become information literate is to understand the information landscape that bounds the setting for practice, and to understand that this knowing is influenced by the processes and practices that are contextually sanctioned. This point is made by Flyvbjerg (2001, p. 42) when he suggests that 'context is important for defining what counts as action'.

In the practice of library and information science research, context is usually briefly described in order to provide a background against which the research object will be explored (Talja *et al.*, 1999). This approach tends to marginalize the role that context plays in framing how a phenomenon is brought into view. However, in information literacy research, understanding how the features and characteristics of a given context shape, form and influence the participant's experience with information becomes an important task for the researcher. Viewing this experience through its context allows us to see what activities and processes influence the nature and manifestation of information literacy. It also allows us to understand which of these are transferable and which have specific temporal and spatial dimensions.

Therefore, the first task for researchers and practitioners becomes the mapping of the context or setting. This is not just as a backdrop that situates the research, and, something that can be forgotten as the researcher focuses on the research object. Context is a central feature that influences and determines the information experience and the range of process and activities that affect the manifestation of information literacy practice.

In defining context, Schatzki (2002, p. xiv) describes it as a 'setting or backdrop that envelops and determines phenomena' and which 'envelops entities' and helps determine their existence and being (Schatzki, 2002, p. 20). According to Schatzki (pp. 61–63), context predetermines practices, which in turn prefigures the types of activities that will occur. It is characterized by three aspects, it:

- embraces and entangles the phenomena;
- shapes the phenomena and entities within it; and
- has composition and character that will vary 'with the entities or phenomena that exist in context'.

This determination has its foundation in social, political and historical arrangements that are laid down and embedded over time and give shape to the context, its discourses and practices. In this respect, what is learnt and how it is learnt; the forms of learning that are legitimized; what information and knowledge is valued; the practices, including information practices, that are legitimized; what subjectivities (knowing self) and intersubjectivities (knowing us) are spoken into existence; and what is contested, are predetermined for those who enter the contextual doors. In the educational landscape, for example, the library-centric view of information literacy that prevails in formal educational settings is the basis of existing information literacy standards and guidelines. This view reflects the types of activities undertaken by librarians, and the skill sets they use, in searching for information that is explicit in that landscape's definitions of an information literate person.

If context predetermines practices, as Schatzki suggests, then understanding the nature of information literacy requires us to explore how people experience information *in context* and how this experience is afforded in relation to the:

- *discourse* (the social actions, including language) of the context, which position a person in particular ways towards modalities of information that characterize in situ (site-specific knowledge) (Schatzki, 2002, p. xiv);

- *affordances* or opportunities furnished within the context, which enable or constrain access to information (Lloyd, 2005); and

- *discursive practices* (actions that are valued and sanctioned) related to information practice that are socially and discursively sanctioned and played out in context.

Discourse

Any account of context must also consider the way discourse and power act as drivers for understanding what information and knowledge is legitimized and which practices and procedures are used to maintain and keep information and knowledge in circulation within a social group. Information and knowledge are not static concepts that are simply acquired, stored and managed, nor are they created in isolation from other practices. They are entwined through the co-participation of people who engage in similar projects or inhabit the same environments and who, because of this engagement with site-specific information and knowledge, develop subject positions in relation to their setting.

Information is data that has been made meaningful through interpretation as a part of an interaction, while knowledge is a mix of codified and embodied information that has been sanctioned over time by the community, which claims it as its own truth and way of knowing. The community tends to it through reflection and reflexivity, constantly adding and positioning it, just as a bowerbird might construct a magnificent bower and thus claim its territory.

The grouping of statements around a set of practices in situ accounts for the discourse of the setting that constitutes the structures and rules for the field of practice. According to Mills (2003, p. 54) a discourse 'is a regulated set of statements which combine with others in predicable ways. Discourse is regulated by a set of rules that leads to the distribution and circulation of certain utterances and statements'. Through discourse, power is exerted, enabling some practices while constraining others.

When we explore information literacy *in context* we are also exploring the enabling and constraining of power. Here the ability to become information literate within a context is influenced by the social, historical and political interests that produce and shape context through its discourses and discursive practices. This is done by setting up rules and conceptual tools for thinking about what counts as information and constitutes knowledge. We are also viewing the way power enables and/or constrains information practice by influencing which activities and skills will be recognized as legitimate and which will not. Therefore, coming to *know* the information environment may be fraught with tensions produced by the contestation of information as it is played out according to discourse and discursive practices. In this respect, some voices will be heard, while others will remain silent or marginalized.

In an education setting, for example, the idea that information literacy is a skill that engages students with content and reflects the skills of the librarians' research process prevails in the thinking of many academic librarians. Consequently, information literacy programmes are often geared towards developing effective information searching and evaluation skills in textual sites. The discourse of information literacy in this setting reflects that of the sector, with an increasing focus on how these skills will be acquired and subsequently measured through assessment. Similarly, in a workplace training setting where the focus is on developing and meeting competency, information literacy while not specifically mentioned will be generally understood as a skill that forms part of a larger competency related to knowledge and skills about effective information use. The emphasis of both these discourses is on the individual and their ability to achieve statable and measurable outcomes as ascribed by the institution.

Power within discourse

In accounting for power, Prus (1999, p. 272) suggests that power is not an 'objective phenomenon' but a 'social, meaningful enacted essence'. In the preparatory stages of learning within educational, workplace or community settings, people connect with epistemic sites of knowledge. Engaging with information, in the form of written rules, practices and procedures, positions newcomers in all sectors in relation to the organizational expectations, allowing them to form an institutionally recognized identity, i.e. they learn *to act as a student/practitioner/ participant*. The transition from the periphery of participation requires engagement with an altered discourse that reflects the social and/or corporeal realities that make up the narrative of the experienced student/practitioner/participant. In the workplace, for example, experienced workplace practitioners play a powerful role in the transition process for newcomers. Power is enacted through discursive practices of the collective who mediate the information environment by guiding novices towards the sites of knowledge that reflect the realities of their workplace practice and performance. By engaging with social and corporeal sites of knowledge, novices are drawn away from the artificial constructs of practice developed in preparatory training, towards collective stories and workplace practices that reflect the realities of their actual work. Through this engagement they are repositioned into the intersubjectively shared constructs of the community of practice, and learn to *become practitioners*.

Information modalities

Discourse maintains the knowledge of the domain, giving it a shape and character, influencing speaking, doing, thinking and acting within a setting. Access to these domains is derived through information modalities: sites where understanding about what constitutes information is shared in addition to the ways in which the community operationalizes this way of knowing. All contexts have a complex set of knowing locations that are interrelated. Here I am defining these very broadly as epistemic (related to objective knowledge), social (related to tacit information) and corporeal (information drawn from bodily learning). These locations are interrogated by participants in the process of learning about the practices of the setting. Depending on the nature of the authority (i.e. its historical, social and political traditions that have helped to shape context over time), these locations will have a varying focus and some locations will be emphasized while others will be contested. In the process of becoming information literate some locations will take precedence and be foregrounded, for example, scientific discourse and the epistemic modality, as the most appropriate for engaging with context over others.

The term information modality describes the broad sites of information that are established within a context. Each of these modalities produces a different experience with information, primarily because the information has a specific quality or dimension (e.g. it is textual, physical or social). Understanding the value of each of these modalities to the learner, how access to this information is operationalized and the outcomes of engaging with each, also provides insights into the type of information experiences that occur and the range of information practices and information skills that facilitate this interaction.

Epistemic modalities

Epistemic modalities act as knowing locations for *know-why* or *know-that* information, which has been codified into written rules and regulations for practice, which can be clearly articulated and evaluated against a set of sanctioned criteria. Information within this modality is used to enact the institutional identity that enables members to be recognized. Universities, schools and training organizations are centralized around epistemic modalities and their information practice, activities and skills are shaped by epistemic forms of knowing, through disciplinary knowledge often seen as fixed and invariable in time and space. From an organizational perspective, this modality reflects the *public face* of the institution or organization, for both employees and the general public. It will be highlighted through the rules, regulations and guidelines for internal and external practice.

In this modality information is tightly bound to institutionally sanctioned forms of knowledge, which can be characterized as theoretical and context independent and underpinned by a 'general analytic rationality' (Flyvbjerg, 2001, p. 15). This modality is distinguished by the use of the written word as text (print or digital). Within this modality information and knowledge are experienced by the user as universal, generalizable and abstract. There is a common belief that truth is objective, discoverable, can be reproduced and is assessable.

As we have seen in previous chapters, an educational conception of information literacy is often reduced to the acquisition and development of a set of skills that relate closely to library literacy or computer literacy programmes and ways of learning and teaching in formal contexts. These are centralized around access to textual sources of information. Therefore, library classes at the minimum will focus on orienting the user within the library and its resources. At the other end, information literacy session training sessions will focus around a set of skills (defining, locating, accessing, evaluating and presenting information) that are intended to support the student in their engagement with textual information. These skills are normally *bolted on* and therefore similar to traditional literacy approaches. However, there have been challenges to this approach and there is an emerging body of thought that advocates for an embedded approach whereby information literacy is taught in relation to the disciplinary content.

The language used to define information literacy connects the phenomenon to the educational setting and is readily understood by teachers and librarians who are stakeholders in the learning process. The emphasis of this concept of information literacy is on developing skills and competencies with information in order to access and evaluate information, to think about information and to demonstrate and document the process of that thinking. The concept as it is viewed in this context is influenced by a rationalist perspective, with an emphasis on print and digital cultures that focus on abstract and immaterial representations of coming to know (Morris and Beckett, 2004). This approach is illustrative of the dominant voices within education, which identify learning as a product (Hager, 2004). It also requires learning outcomes to be demonstrated and assessed against a standard measurement and aligned with a construct of what a good student should be or, in our case, what an information literate person should be. In an educational setting information literacy emerges as a tangible set of processes and the development of a set of skills and attributes that characterize an information literate person.

In this respect, information is discursively produced and its use promoted by specific communities that represent particular ideological positions, values, beliefs and attitudes. Textbooks, guidelines, standards and procedural documents are examples of epistemic genres. Engaging with these modalities produces a subjective position in relation to the codified, objective information that is sanctioned by the institution or organization.

Social modalities

The social modality is constituted through accounts of action and social interaction and produce embodied *know-how* or tacit knowledge (Ryle, 1949). This type of information is sourced from the situated experiences of collective participation, practice and reflection on action. Social information is drawn from an individual's personal biography as well as collective histories of people in shared practice. Foundational to this modality is experiential information, and information that represents the real and ongoing values and beliefs of participants in practice. Consequently, in this modality information is fluid and the ways of knowing are constantly changing. Social information is difficult to articulate though text but is highly valued by the collective because it shapes the initial subjectivities and then enables the enacting of intersubjectivity once members engage with the actual practice of the setting. This allows them to move from the reified identity produced through engagement with epistemic information (learning to act) towards the construction of a collective identity (becoming).

This type of information is located within and through the community of practice with which an individual connects, and it is through this modality that information about working culture and identity are shared (Brown and Duguid, 2001). Social information has both subjective and intersubjective dimensions that are intertwined.

For newcomers to a community, access to social information provides an explanatory framework from which to construct a sense of place and a perspective on practice. This enables them to begin the process of reshaping identity from an institutional identity, gained through initial access to the epistemic modality, towards enacting a collective workplace identity that reflects the shared understandings about practice. The negotiation of collective identity occurs through access to information that is rich in its historical, political and social contribution to the maintenance of community perspective. This modality can be further categorized into two dimensions.

■ *Personal dimension of social information*. In this dimension, personal information produces subjectivity. This type of information is drawn from personal observation about one's own practice and personal history (ontogeny). It is informed by experiences (or lack of experiences), and can be drawn from engaging with epistemic sites that outline the rules of action. These experiences produce an identity that reflects the institutional expectations of practice.

- *Collective information.* Participating in shared frameworks of practice and ways of interpreting the world is facilitated by the community of practice, which gradually *draws in* the newcomer from the boundaries of practice toward the community of practice and enables the transformation from peripheral participation towards full participation (Lave and Wenger, 1991). This participation enables the newcomer or novice to begin engaging with an intersubjective space that is controlled by others. The discourse influencing this modality is situated and constituted over time by historical, political and social motivations that shape the storyline and narratives of the collective and the practices it produces and values.

In this respect social modalities are context-dependent and value-laden in relation to truth and competing interests. This modality is also variable, pragmatic and action oriented (Flyvbjerg, 2001, p. 57). Social modalities, therefore, are intrinsically based in experience and act as a source of situated knowledge. This modality can be thought of as the knowing location from which wisdom about practice and culture are derived, rather than the location of axiomatic truth. Social modalities are closely associated with reflection and reflexivity about professional practice and professional identity.

This type of information is accessed through the storylines of the community and the stories of individuals within the community. Sondergaard (2002, p. 191) describes storylines as '... a condensed version of a naturalised and conventional cultural narrative, one that is often used as the explanatory framework of one's own and other's practices and sequences of action'. Deconstruction of narrative and storytelling, provides newcomers with access to information that draws them away from the periphery to which they have been brought by their institutional learning, towards the community, allowing them to develop or reinforce a sense of place, and a perspective on practice. Social information is richly historical, political and cultural and therefore makes a critical contribution to the reinforcement and maintenance of community perspective.

Corporeal modality

The corporeal modality is formed through experience and manifests as information that is embodied and situated. It is, therefore, a context-dependent modality that acts as a knowing location for know-how information or practical knowledge (Ryle, 1949; Billett, 2001). This type of information is tacit, or contingent, and it is disseminated through demonstration and observation of practice or accessed through the tactile and kinaesthetic activity associated with actual practice. Corporeal information cannot be easily articulated or expressed explicitly, and, when it is, it is only partially explicit (Blackler, 1995). I have previously (2006, p. 575) argued that bodies reflect the consciousness of engagement with information. They act as a collector of sensory information, a site of knowledge and as a disseminator of physical experience. The body in action provides its own narrative that must be observed through practice. In performance the body becomes the intersection between epistemic information, information drawn from actual performance and information drawn from interaction with the community of practice.

Information from the corporeal domain, accessed through the senses and the action of the body of others, provides the baseline for embodied practice and leads to intersubjective constructions about the collective life of practice and profession. According to O'Loughlin (1998, p. 279) bodies are 'not simply subject to external agency, but are simultaneously agents in their socio-construction of the world'. Bodies are therefore used as a source of sensory and sentient information gathering, as an instrument of non-verbal communication about practice and as a symbol of community that reflects the discourse in which the body is situated socially, politically and historically.

Information from this site is critical for the construction of meaningful practice and corresponds to Merleau-Ponty's (1962) account of the *lived body* as the centre and symbol of learning and experience and the development of intersubjectivity in collective practice. For Merleau-Ponty bodies become storehouses of information and understandings that find a commonality of shared meanings within the culture. Intersubjective meaning is created through the perception of commonality, which suggests that embodiment is culturally produced (O'Loughlin. 1998).

Accounting for the body in the construction of knowledge, Dewey emphasizes the *social body* and the sociality of experience through bodily interaction, which leads to intersubjective conceptions of practice and profession. Dewey's conception of the social body is highlighted by O'Loughlin (1998, p. 286) when she states that:

> Meaning which is always socially produced emerged from embodied co-operative human activity. By ongoing participation in

the activities of the group, the weaving of relationship among its members, body subjects learn to respond with habitual orientations to the changed stimuli of their environments. Embodied communication is the way in which over time people grasp things in common and come to partake of communication in a common understanding.

Goffman (1983) also emphasizes the role of the body in social interaction. According to this author, the body plays a central role in the generation of meaning by providing visual information cues about roles and practices, which lead to the establishment of shared vocabularies and meanings, which facilitate embodied knowing.

By observing the bodies of other people in practice, as they rehearse or are in action, we are able to access information that can be used in reflections about the veracity of our own practices. Drawing information from the body organizes the mind through the coupling of formal statements about work, which are predicable and articulated as rules and codes for practice, against uncertain bodily experience. These cannot be articulated or written down as procedure, because it must be experienced and transformed into information and then constructed as knowledge.

In the fire fighter study cited in Chapter 4 the use of physical information to develop *fire sense* has parity with the miners' development of pit sense (Sauer, 1998; Somerville, 2002). Research by Sauer (1998) identified that miners' development of *pit sense* was gained through sensory information that could not be articulated through text. This research also concluded that while 'miners may draw on previous training and experience; they do not call on texts at the moment of action to help them react. Nor do they record their reactions in written communications' (Sauer, 1998, p. 161). Like pit sense, *fire sense* is 'physical and sensory knowledge in the most literal of senses' (Sauer, 1998, p. 137). Somerville's (2002) study of miners reinforces the idea of 'embodied situated knowledge' (p. 46), which originate through physical experiences and become embedded in social practices and traditions. Embodied knowledge is valued as a significant information source as opposed to epistemic or paper knowledge because it has evolved through the complex interaction between the 'worker's body and the place of work' (Somerville, 2005, p. 19).

An awareness of the body as an important source of information in manual labour is also evident in the work of Veinot (2007). In keeping with practice theory, this author accounts for the body of a vault inspector in her description of workplace information practice. In describing the safety protection clothing worn by these vault inspectors, Veinot (2007) also draws attention to these workers' awareness of corporeal information and the vital contribution it makes to embodied performance.

In the initial stages of training or learning to work, the physical modality is an action space through which an individual's interaction produces an individual subjectivity in relation to performance and practice. That is, novices learn *how to act as a practitioner*, but at this preliminary stage they cannot *become a practitioner*, because they lack the experiential grounding that comes from actual practice. However, as interaction with the workplace environment and with the community of practice increases, corporeal information, which is grounded in the experiences of the body in action, also grounds intersubjectivity (Sheets-Johnstone, 2000). As novices interact with the bodies of other workers they develop a mutuality of understanding, which reflects the collective understandings of how practice and the performance of work should proceed.

Through interaction with other actors within context, the novice body is drawn in and turned towards the community of practice. Sheets-Johnstone (2000, p. 344) draws on the concept of joint attention to describe how learning is a corporeal and/or kinetic relationship, which grounds intersubjectivity and is at the heart of novice learning. Joint attention is the result of the body being turned towards other situated bodies. This occurs when novices are located initially on the periphery of a community of practice. In their preparatory learning, novices' bodies are turned towards the community in a number of ways (e.g. through rehearsal and by observation of others).

In summary, information is located within modalities, each with distinctive characteristics that influence ways of knowing and reinforcing the practices and procedures that enable knowing about context to occur. Therefore, within an epistemic modality ways of knowing may focus on disciplinary knowledge that is factual, with information-related activities being benchmarked against criteria and standards (e.g. know-why knowledge). In social modalities, ways of knowing will focus on intersubjectively shared understandings that are tacit, and nuanced and that may contest epistemic knowledge. Formal benchmarking will not occur, but may take the form of *social benchmarking* through acceptance within the group. Corporeal information is embodied and knowing focuses on know-how, where information practices will take the shape of physical activity such as rehearsal, observation and informal benchmarking will take the form of acceptance of performance.

Information practice

Information literacy is a practice that is constituted through a constellation of *affordances*, *information activities* and *skills*, which together enable a way of knowing the modalities of information that constitute an information environment. It is a collaborative practice because the experience of information occurs in a setting and in consort with other people, as well as with the signs, symbols and artefacts of the setting. While engaging with a community of practice will enable an individual to learn about practice, the main purpose of this engagement is more than this: the object is to become a full participant in practice (Fenwick, 2006). This means that the community must provide a range of information affordances that will enable a new member to become engaged with a range of information activities and to develop information skills that are grounded in the 'cultural norms of interactions, methods of practice, identities, and divisions of labour and power' (Fenwick, 2006, p. 699). Therefore, information affordances play an important part in the production of identity, of understanding about practice and performance and development of a sense of place and as such they are important when considering information literacy practice from a holistic perspective. Consequently, when we account for information literacy in our research and teaching, we need to consider not only the most visible form of the practice (i.e. activities and skills) but also the collaborative elements that are employed within a setting. These elements enable new members to engage with the modalities of information and ways of knowing that are part of the sanctioning and operationalizing of practice.

Affordance

The drawing in of the individuals towards co-participation occurs through affordance. These are understood as activities and interactions and defined here as 'invitational opportunities' (Billett *et al.*, 2004) furnished by the environment. According to Gibson (1979), who first coined the term, affordances focus on the sources of information available to people (e.g. symbols and artefacts) available within an environment. In discussing the definition of affordance, Gibson (1979, p. 27) suggests that: 'the affordances of the environment are what it offers the animals, what it provides or furnishes, either for good or ill.' Affordances are therefore opportunities that the setting provides, which promote interaction and action. Gibson's (1979) use of the term relates to the perception of artefacts and symbols that characterize an environment and the meaning that people, who are engaged with that environment, attribute to them. Therefore, an affordance must be perceived as information that is meaningful or that makes a difference. Affordances are contextual, but they are not a prerequisite for action unless they are meaningfully recognized by the participants within the context (Gibson, 1979; Barnes, 2000; Lloyd-Zantiotis, 2004).

Affordances furnish information, and in relation to information literacy, they can be classified as textual, social, and physical. *Textual* affordances are those opportunities that allow members to engage with the codified knowledge of the institution or organization enabling them to come to know the institutional landscape and its accepted practices. *Social* affordances are found in the interactional opportunities that occur between members as they negotiate a shared understanding about information and practice (i.e. a sense of collaborative identity and place). Through co-participation members are afforded information about the collaborative nature of professional practice (i.e. the nature of relationships between members). The information afforded is implicit and nuanced, reflecting the shared values, beliefs and norms of the community of practice. Occasionally this information will conflict with the institutional affordances provided to members when they first engage with the institution. *Physical* affordances manifest through an engagement with the signs, symbols and tools and physical environments of practice. These affordances provide opportunities for members to develop, connect and become reflexive with embodied or contingent information that is closely related to the know-how aspect of performance and cannot be adequately articulated in written form.

Like information, the relationship between the affordance and the information has to be understood as meaningful and useful to particular practices (Chemero, 2003). This suggests that affordance must be understood situationally, as part of the information experience and as forming an ongoing part of knowledge construction. Examples of activities that afford opportunities to connect with information may include guiding, mentoring, rehearsal, scaffolding, modelling or coaching, narration and storytelling (Gibson, 1979; Billett 2001; Lloyd, 2005). Affordances may enable access to embodied information relating to experiences about practice. Most importantly, for an affordance to be taken up by an individual, that individual must perceive the opportunity, which suggests that the value of the affordance (which might be a resource, a tool, or a person or a piece of information) must be recognized by the individual.

When we consider affordances as part of an architecture for information literacy practice we need to account for how the range of information activities occur within a setting and how and why a person interacts and forms relationships with symbols, artefacts or environmental stimuli, including people within an information environment. Having said that, it is also important to understand that the provision or opportunities to engage with information are not evenly distributed or made available to everyone within a setting and not everyone who participates will be given the same or similar opportunities to engage and experience the information environment. In the workplace, for example, access to information affordances may be affected by the nature of work, e.g. differences between part-time workers and full-time workers or novice and expert workers, or the contesting of practice between the two groups. In other settings, such as libraries, access to affordances may be affected by librarians' perception of their clients or librarians' conception of themselves as gatekeepers. In an educational setting, opportunities to access information may be a teacher's perceptions of students' abilities or need for information.

The nature of the activities and desired outcomes will influence what affordances are valued and how they are offered through co-participatory practice and used by participants. From the perspective of information literacy practice, affordances can be conceived as information experienced in the landscape, through formal, informal or incidental information seeking and dissemination activities, which encourage an individual to become reflective and reflexive about their practices and then draw individuals into membership.

In educational contexts, affordances may occur through the librarian–student interaction and be centrally focused around engaging with the online world through computer instruction (to access databases or catalogues) or instruction about analysing and evaluating textual sources (print and information and communication technology literacy) specific to the student's discipline knowledge. In workplaces, affordances may be centrally focused on engaging and guiding the newcomer through the opportunities offered in the storylines of the community of practice. They may also provide opportunities for novices to engage with tacit and contingent sources of knowledge, which cannot be articulated or expressed in textual form but are still central to developing knowledge about practice and work performance.

Interacting with sources of information that are afforded within the context facilitates meaning making and allows the individual to develop an individual subjective position (the individual as learner) and, over time, an intersubjective position in relation to others who act in consort as a community of practice. In this respect, activities including information seeking and information dissemination, are enmeshed and shaped within context, and facilitate information engagement and experience. This enables the individual to move towards participation in the performance of meaning making activities, including engaging with signs and symbols that are valued by the community and by making connections with others already engaged with the community.

Information activities

Practices are composed of a number of interwoven activities within a given social domain (Schatzki, 1997). In relation to information literacy, a number of activities are identifiable that contribute to its architecture. In some of the literature these activities are often described as practices; however, there has been little detailed reflection about what would constitute these 'information practices', i.e. what constellation of activities and skills would characterize them (Savolainen, 2007). Therefore, for the purpose of this information literacy architecture, information activities are described as purposeful ways of doing things, influenced by the discourse of the landscape (the sayings), which been sanctioned at an institutional or a social level or both.

Information work

Information work is a situational activity. In other attempts to define this activity, information work has been discussed, as it is operationalized by the individual in 'dealing with purposive, conscious and intended actions' and focusing on what is done with information (Savolainen, 2007, p. 123). In the context of information literacy practice and of this architecture, information work refers to the strategies that are employed not only by members but also the collective strategies of the community to ensure that all members engage with information, sites of knowledge and employ appropriate information skills, which reflect the ways of doing things as sanctioned by the community. The way in which information work is operationalized will depend on the way information and knowledge are understood by the domain, and this in turn will influence the type of activities that occur and become legitimized. For example, in the emergency services studies (Lloyd, 2007) the flow of information is managed by the institutions. Novices were not encouraged to go outside of their training settings in order to access information about practice. Rather, they were corralled within the confines of their training organizations and provided with information that was considered relevant to their preparatory training. The formation of epistemic barriers that act to keep members within the confines of the knowledge domain or alternatively to act as a barrier to outsiders, is a common feature of communities of practice, noted in the work of Brown and Duguid (1991) and Wenger (1998).

Experts and newcomers alike perform information work as they engage in collaborative participation. Information work may be constituted through the *epistemic modality* as the development of activities and strategies that engage members with sources of codified knowledge. Activities may include members' skill development in searching, organizing, analysing, evaluating and presenting information. Strategies may relate to reflection of content, and a reflexive view about the application of information skills.

Within a *social modality* information work may be constituted through the mapping of appropriate relationships within the community and may involve judgements about trust and reliability that will be assessed against nuanced information. However, mapping is not just an intra-community activity, the mapping of socially distributed networks also becomes important, particularly to experienced members who will search for salience, which they can use to inform and improve their own practice as well as the practices of the community as a whole.

Demonstration engages novices with information about the range of actions required in professional practice. Demonstration allows the new members to situate the body in relation to the expectations and standards required of the practice. It allows experienced members to mediate information in relation to the action or performance and at the same time turns new members' bodies towards joint attention that will produce a shared focus that in early stages is preparatory. This activity allows the body to be signified by other practitioners as a novice body. Rehearsal of demonstrated practices affords new members with an opportunity to develop a suite of bodily actions that may mirror those of experts, but is still unconnected to the realities and uncertainties of actual practice. For intersubjectivity to develop, bodies must be physically turned towards one another. In the early stages of novice learning, epistemic, social and physical modalities prepare the novice bodies for perfunctory performance, but they cannot prepare them for the uncertainties of practice.

Influence work

The community plays a critical role in facilitating the transition of new members towards co-participation and shared practice. The community acts as a site for access to information by mediating the information landscape and wider environment on their behalf. Influence work describes how the community actively engages the new member in the negotiation about identity and ways of interpreting practice. In undertaking this activity the community actively shapes:

- the ways in which information is understood by its members;
- access to the sources of information that are considered valuable to informing practice; and
- the ways in which information is disseminated and shared.

As part of an information strategy, influence work aims at repositioning new members towards the community and the renegotiations of their identity.

Communities of practice are essentially informal and define themselves according to the way they engage in practice (e.g. learning practice, work practice or community practice). This concept of practice differs considerably from the reified and abstract concept of institutional practice that new members engage with as part of their initial membership. This point is made by Wenger (1998, p. 119) when he suggests that 'the landscape of practice is therefore not congruent with the reified structures of institutional affiliations, divisions, and boundaries. It is not independent of these institutional structures, but neither is it reducible to them'.

Through experience of interaction with other members and through the actual performance of work, information is grounded and subsequently meaning making takes on an intersubjective shape. Membership of a community of practice requires the production and reproduction of identity. The aim of influence work is to create an intersubjectively constituted reality about practice and procedure through the mediation and interpretation of information as it is experienced in actual practice. Influence work may emerge as the narration of events, story telling or interpretation of procedural materials. It is also constituted through the mediating and interpreting activities that occur within a setting. From a corporeal level it may manifest through activities such as the demonstration of embodied experience.

Information sharing

The activity of information sharing is central to both *information work* and *influence work*. This feature has not been considered in relation to information literacy research, nor has it been widely researched in the library and information sector. Where this is the case, it is often referred to as an information practice (Talja and Hansen, 2005). However, in the framework of practice that has been employed for this work, information sharing is understood not as a practice but as an activity that is purposeful and one that is affected and influenced by the *sayings and doings* of the environment. Information sharing is a purposeful activity, which enables a member to give and receive information. When it is considered in the light of collaborative socio-cultural practices it is the receipt of information that is of interest because this affects the information and influences work that occurs within information literacy practice.

Coupling

As a central activity of information literacy practice, coupling is the process by which information from the textual sites, from bodily experience of authentic practice and from the socially nuanced site are drawn together and render the member 'in place' within the intersubjective space. Coupling facilitates emergent awareness of where information is situated, and the strategies used to operationalize access to it within the various modalities.

Becoming information literate, knowing the information landscape and its access points characterizes the embodied practice that renders the individual in place and facilitates the transfer from subjectivity to intersubjectivity. Engaging with information through the situated information modalities via the affordances of experienced members in the setting enables new members to connect with the intersubjective framework of established practice and identity and as well as with the collectively agreed ways of knowing. Coupling is central in the transition from peripheral to embodied practitioner. It is attended to through the affordances (information and influence work) in which information accessed from textual, social and corporeal sites are drawn together and render the newcomer in place.

Coupling engages the institutional knower with the physical and social sites of knowledge and facilitates the transition from *acting* to *becoming*.

Through coupling of the mind, body and experience, the institutional knower is positioned by the affordances of the community that influence the actions and activities required in practice.

Conclusion

In describing the architecture for information literacy as a socio-cultural practice we need to account for the many layers that influence and make that practice possible. Information literacy is not simply a matter of applying and demonstrating skills. It is more than this, it is being literate about the information landscapes and environments that a person inhabits and recognizing that people construct these spaces over time in an ongoing attempt to maintain and manage specific cultural and social formations. Consequently, they are prefigured and shaped by social, historical, material and political conditions that influence the way information is understood and knowledge is ultimately constructed. To be an informed and knowing user of an information environment requires us to understand how and why information and knowledge are constructed and maintained in addition to an understanding of where information is located.

Conceptualizing an architecture of information literacy allows us to account for the socio-cultural aspects that influence its manifestation and practice and enables information literacy to act as a catalyst for learning in all contexts. Critical features of this architecture include recognition of:

- the influence of context on the prefiguration and shaping of information modalities within a setting; and
- the role of information affordances in enabling access to information about practices and the activities that facilitate information literacy within context.

Implications for information literacy education

Information literacy is a situated socio-cultural practice that informs other practices and in doing so enables understanding and intelligibility to occur. It is constituted through a range of information activities and information skills that are operationalized within a community. By constructing an architecture for information literacy we are able to make explicit the key features of this practice.

The concept of information literacy must be understood through its use. This suggests that an understanding of how information literacy as practice is situated within a social site becomes a critical first step in developing effective pedagogy. As I suggested in an earlier chapter, educational institutions are preparatory. They prepare people to enter work or to participate in the community. To be effective in this task, librarians and information literacy educators must be able to recognize how practice is constituted outside their own field and account for this in their teaching practice. This is a big task at the best of times and for library educators it can be incredibly difficult, given the tensions that they must contend with in relation to their status, often not as faculty, and with limited resources. But try we must!

The architecture I have proposed here takes the concepts of practice and situatedness and attempts to identify the key features for information literacy that will be present in all contexts. It does not focus on skills because the development of skills is, I believe, a situated practice that needs to be understood, as it is operationalized, rather than be determined by librarians who may lack a broader understanding of information practice outside of their own setting. The architecture is not perfect and should be an ongoing construction as more research and thinking about information literacy across a range of settings is conducted. It should not be followed slavishly, but it should encourage you to think about the role of information literacy education and how you might prepare students for the world outside the library or the classroom.

There are implications of this approach for the library and information science profession and for librarians who champion information literacy. For library and information science educators:

- there is an greater need to include training and education for information literacy within their own courses to ensure that all librarians recognize the complexity of information literacy, and have the ability to account for this complexity in the development of their programmes;

- there is a need for us to cast beyond our own literature in order to enrich our understandings about how information is experienced and used, and thus improve our ability to develop information literacy pedagogy for our students in ways that can account for the complexity and richness of the practice; and

- there is a need to theorize information literacy as practice, and as such to seek and test a range of theoretical frameworks through which information literacy can be described.

For librarians and information literacy educators there is a need to:

- recast information literacy as a socio-cultural practice and to develop programmes that not only focus on library-centric skills but also on communication skills;

- develop programmes that enable critical thinking not only within the context of the education setting, but also critical thinking about the *how* and *why* of information, as it is communicated orally and physically;

- recognize the issues that surround situated learning, and to consider how we best prepare students to learn using a range of information modalities that may be unfamiliar to those of us who are bound in a textual and digital world;

- recognition of the role that social information plays in the shaping of information literacy practice; and

- recognition of the body as a source of information and inclusion of this modality in information literacy instruction.

The research into workplace information literacy highlights that the current behaviour and skills approach is not suitable for wider settings. If information literacy is to truly underpin notions of lifelong learning then librarians and information literacy educators need to understand the broader conception of information literacy as a collaborative practice and work towards students and clients developing skills and approaches to information that are not solely focused around text, but also include oral communication skills and visual skills, such as observation. They also need to develop in students the ability to become reflective and reflexive practitioners who are able to critically assess and question not only the information but also the conditions through which it is provided.

References

Barnes, S. (2000). What does electronic conferencing afford distance education? *Distance Education*, 21(2), 226–247.

Billett, S. (2001). *Learning in the workplace: strategies for effective practice*. Crows Nest, NSW, Australia: Allen & Unwin.

Billett, S., Barker, M. and Hernon-Tinning, B. (2004). Participatory practices at work. *Pedagogy, Culture and Society*, 12(2), 233–257.

Blackler, F. (1995). Knowledge, knowledge work and organizations: An overview and interpretation. *Organization Studies*, 16(6), 1021–1046.

Brown, J. S. and Duguid, P. (1991). Organizational learning and communities of practice: toward a unified view of working, learning and innovation. *Organizational Science*, 2(1), 40–57.

Chemero, A. (2003). An outline of a theory of affordances. *Ecological Psychology*, 15(2), 181–195.

Dervin, B. (1996).Given a context by any other name: Methodological tools for taming the unruly beast. In P. Vakkari, R. Savolainen and B. Dervin (eds.), *Information seeking in context* (pp. 13–38). London: Taylor Graham.

Fenwick, T. (2006). Learning as grounding and flying: knowledge, skill and transformation in changing work contexts. *Journal of Industrial Relations*, 48, 691–706.

Flyvbjerg, B. (2001). *Making social science matter; why social inquiry fails and how it can succeed again.* Cambridge: Cambridge University Press.

Gibson, J. J. (1979). *The ecological approach to visual perception.* Boston, MA: Houghton Mifflin.

Goffman, E. (1983). The interaction order. *American Sociological Review*, 48, 1–17.

Hager, P. (2004). Lifelong learning in the workplace? Challenges and issues. *Journal of Workplace learning*, 16(1/2), 22–32.

Hager, P. and Smith, E. (2004). The inescapability of significant contextual learning in work performance. *London Review of Education*, 2(1), 33–46.

Kemmis, S. and Grootenboer, P. (2008). Situating praxis in practice. In S. Kemmis and T. J. Smith (Eds), *Enabling Praxis* (pp. 37–62). Rotterdam: Sense Publishers.

Lave, J. and Wenger, E. (1991). *Situated learning: legitimate peripheral participation.* New York: Cambridge University Press.

Lincoln, Y. and Guba, E. (2003). Paradigmatic controversies, contradictions, and emerging confluences. In N. K. Denzin and Y. Lincoln (Eds), *The landscape of qualitative research: theories and issues* (2nd ed.). Thousand Oaks, CA: Sage Publications.

Lloyd, A. (2005). No man (or woman) is an island: information literacy, affordances and communities of practice. *Australian Library Journal*, 54(3), 230–237.

Lloyd, A. (2006). Information literacy landscapes: an emerging picture. *Journal of Documentation*, 62(5), 570–583.

Lloyd, A. (2007). Recasting information literacy as sociocultural practice: implications for library and information science researchers.

Information Research, 12(4). Retrieved 10 November 2008 from http://InformationR.net/ir/12-4/colis34.html/.

Lloyd-Zantiotis, A. (2004). *Working information: a grounded theory of information literacy in the workplace.* Unpublished Doctoral Dissertation, University of New England, Armidale, NSW.

Merleau-Ponty, M. (1962). *Phenomenology of perception.* London: Routledge and Kegan Paul.

Mills, S. (2003). *Michel Foucault.* London: Routledge.

Morris, G. and Beckett, D. (2004). Learning for/at work: Somali women 'doing it for themselves'. *Journal of Workplace Learning*, 16 (1/2), 75–82.

O'Loughlin, M. (1998). Paying attention to bodies in education: theoretical resources and practical suggestions. *Educational Philosophy and Theory*, 30(3), 275–297.

Prus, R. (1999). Beyond the power mystique: power as intersubjective accomplishment. Albany, NY: State University of New York Press.

Ryle, G. (1949). *The concept of mind.* London: Hutchinson University Library.

Sauer, B. (1998). Embodied knowledge: the textual representation of embodied sensory information in a dynamic and uncertain material environment. *Written Communication*, 15(2), 131–169.

Savolainen, R. (2007). Information behaviour and information practice; reviewing the 'umbrella concepts' of information seeking studies. *Library Quarterly*, 77(2), 109–132.

Schatzki, T. (1997). Practices and actions: a Wittgensteinian critique of Bourdieu and Giddens. *Philosophy of the Social Sciences*, 27(3), 283–308.

Schatzki, T. (2002). *The site of the social: a philosophical account of the constitution of social life and change.* Pennsylvania, PA: Pennsylvania University Press.

Sheets-Johnstone, M. (2000). Kinetic tactile-kinesthetic bodies: ontogenetical foundations of apprenticeship learning. *Human Studies*, 23, 343–370.

Somerville, M. (2002). *Masculine workplace cultures and learning safety in the mining industry.* Armidale, NSW: School of Adult and Workplace Education, Faculty of Education, University of New England.

Somerville, M. (2005). Working culture: exploring notions of workplace culture and learning at work. *Pedagogy, Culture and Society*, 13(1), 5–26.

Sondergaard, D. M. (2002). Poststructural approaches to empirical analysis. *Qualitative Studies in Education*, 15(2), 187–204.

Talja, S. and Hansen, P. (2005). Information sharing. In A. Spink and C. Cole (Eds), *New directions in human information behaviour* (pp. 113–134). Berlin: Springer.

Talja, S., Keso, H. and Pietilainen, T. (1999). The production of 'context' in information seeking research; a metatheoretical view. *Information Processing and Management, 35,* 751–763.

Veinot, T. (2007). The eyes of the power company: workplace information practices of a vault inspector. *Library Quarterly,* 77(2), 157–179.

Wenger, E. (1998). *Communities of practice: learning, meaning and identity.* Cambridge: Cambridge University Press.

8

Concluding comments

Information literacy is a powerful concept with pedagogic, economic and social implications. However, with a few notable exceptions in the education field (Bruce, 1996; Lupton, 2008) this recognition has not translated into attempts to theorize information literacy as an overarching information practice that has the power to explain the interplay between information, people and context. Instead a more applied approach that is centralized around the operationalization of library and computer skills has been the focus.

Wiegand (1999) has previously noted that librarians (and I include information literacy researchers) tend to be trapped within the discursive formation of their profession, a profession that is largely atheoretical and inward looking. In relation to information literacy, the profession is more focused on developing generic library skills rather than understanding the nature of information literacy practice and the ongoing social processes that enable it. If information literacy is truly a prerequisite for lifelong learning and a core literacy in the twenty-first century (Garner, 2006) then serious attention needs to be paid to other circumstances, settings and ways of knowing that do not reflect the textually bound conceptions of information literacy currently dominating the literature. Subsequently, discussions about information literacy need to acknowledge the co-participatory processes that draw members towards situated knowledge within a setting, and the reflexive and embodied learning that occurs when people co-participate in practice.

Information literacy is bound and made visible through its situatedness, suggesting that it is inextricably tied to context. It gains meaning through the way it manifests as actions and activities, centred on information, which are shaped and prefigured by historical, social, cultural, economic and political dimensions. To understand information literacy requires us to understand how context is prefigured and how this prefigurement shapes information and knowledge and the activities that are used to access and share these. It requires us to understand the interconnections between people, practice, information, knowledge and the world as constructed. In this respect information literacy is a situated practice that is shaped through the interactions between people. This explains why it is so difficult to articulate a single definition for information literacy because each definition is a product of its particular setting with its underlying discourse about what information is and what forms of knowledge are legitimate.

Therefore, although important to an overall understanding of information literacy, we should abandon attempts to define the phenomenon with reference to a generic suite of skills. Instead, information literacy should be explained with reference to its outcomes and to the socio-cultural features that operationalize the constellation of activities and skills that have been recognized and sanctioned according to the social, historical, political and economic arrangements that are heritaged within a particular site.

This book has approached information literacy from a specific theoretical framework and introduced social and practice theory in order to frame it as a socio-cultural practice. It has explored information literacy across a number of landscapes to illustrate the various ways in which the phenomenon has been conceptualized by library and information researchers and practitioners. In doing so, it has attempted to identify some of the themes that prevail in literature. In addition to this, it has also attempted to highlight the problematic nature of our current ways of describing this complex phenomenon and has advocated the need to adopt a contextualist approach to our research into this area. By framing the critical features that influence information literacy, an architecture is proposed that accounts for social process and features that should be considered as an integral part of research. These features should also be considered when developing pedagogy around information literacy and included in teaching as a way of encouraging students to think critically not just about the search for information but also how information is constituted through the settings that are searched.

To understand information literacy, we need to think about it holistically, not simply in terms of how an individual engages with the written word, but more broadly, in recognizing that other modalities of information are important and lead to the development of practical understandings and knowledge. We also need to recognize that information literacy is not an individual pursuit. It is performed in consort with situated others who have a vested interested in ensuring that information activities and skills reflect sanctioned socio-cultural, technical and material practices. It also ensures that a new member's experience with information produces intelligibility and understanding of the situated practices required as part of the enactment into practice.

To this end, we need to account for the types of information and knowledge that are valued within a setting and how they are valued. We need to account for the activities that are used to impart the value of information and knowledge to members and for the information activities and skills that are sanctioned. Finally, we need to consider the outcomes of information literacy practice.

By reframing information literacy through socio-cultural and practice theory this book attempts to theorize information literacy by demonstrating its complex nature as a situated practice that produces specific ways of knowing, and accounting for the collaborative and contextual nature of information literacy as a situated practice. Through this frame information literacy can be seen as a suite of affordances and information activities that facilitate engaging with information located within discourse, other practices and tools of particular settings. By interaction with others in the setting, members are able to share and negotiate an understanding of and about information, leading to the development of intersubjectivity. As a holistic practice, becoming information literate necessitates not only access to codified sources, but also access to embodied information.

Put simply, information literacy is a way of knowing about the sources of information that inform practice. However, in reality information literacy practice is underpinned by a rich complexity because the concept of information is not simple nor is it unproblematic and ways of knowing are not always easy but are often contested and fraught with tension. Our job as information literacy researchers, as librarians and as educators is to develop our understanding of this complexity, and the way it influences information literacy as a situated socio-cultural practice within a landscape, so we can reconceptualize our own practices and pedagogy.

References

Bruce, C. (1996). *Information literacy; a phenomenography.* Unpublished Doctoral Dissertation, University of New England, Armidale, NSW, Australia.

Garner, S. (2006). Report of a Meeting Sponsored by the United Nations Educational, Scientific and Cultural Organization (UNESCO), National Forum on Information Literacy (NFIL) and the International Federation of Library Associations and Institutions (IFLA). Retrieved 30 November 2008, http://www.ifla.org/III/wsis/High-Level\Colloquium .pdf/.

Lupton, M. (2008). *Information literacy and learning*. Unpublished Doctoral Dissertation, Queensland University of Technology.

Wiegand, W.A. (1999). Tunnel vision and blind spots: what the past tells us about the present: reflections on the twentieth-century history of American librarianship. *Library Quarterly*, 69(1), 1–32.

Index

Lightning Source UK Ltd.
Milton Keynes UK
UKOW06f0649120615

253385UK00010B/275/P